SPRING UP
O WELL

SPRING UP O WELL

RELEASING THE TRANSFORMATIVE POWER OF PROPHECY

DWAYNE HOWARD

Foreword by Stephen Holford

Spring Up O Well

KAINOS^{cs}

Published by Kainos Creative Studios Inc.
www.kainoscs.com

For permissions or more information contact info@kainoscs.com.

Unless otherwise stated, all Scripture quoted has been taken from the New King James Version®. Copyright © 1982 by Thomas Nelson. Used by permission. All rights reserved.

Cover Design, Book Design and Layout by Kainos Creative Studios Inc.
Editing and proofreading services provided by Kainos Creative Studios Inc.

ISBN Print 978-976-96568-5-7 | Epub 978-976-96568-6-4 | PDF 978-976-96568-7-1

Dedication

I've dedicated this book to a very special person that God sent my way when I was just seventeen years old. She has served for over thirty years as the Aglow International Southern Area Board President, and is also a minister at her local church which is nestled in the beautiful island of Barbados. She is such an amazing example not just in ministry  but family, having been married now for over 64 years, and presides over a family that loves and cherishes her golden heart. Her name is Agnes Niccolls and I'd like to share some of our story with you.

If the journey in answering God's call upon my life unfolded like episodes of a TV show in its first season, Agnes Niccolls would be one of the featured and most prominent characters of that show outside of God Himself. She played a major role in me saying yes to what He had in store for my life. She saw the prophetic gifting that resided within me, called it forth, and mentored me through my first steps of being faithful to the call. Without her, I would have never made it out of the first few episodes of destiny, and I am eternally grateful for her contribution. She willingly provided me with all the resources I needed and continually fanned the flame of God on the inside of me with constant encouragement to the call and discernment in addressing matters of my heart. Even before I knew who the great Dr. Bill Hamon was, her library of his books became my own, and little did I know that God would have me leave my pursuit of aeronautical engineering to attend Dr. Bill's ministry training college in Florida two years later. In this we see God's divine providence, that even when we cannot trace Him we can confidently trust Him, as He is ordaining every step for our good.

I remember the initial moment when our paths crossed as if it were yesterday. Our church, New Dimensions Ministries, was hosting their weekly Friday night service and the Presence of God flooded the room. It was so incredibly overwhelming that all that transpired was worship that evening. I was completely undone by the atmosphere of God's Presence, and it was then that as I cried out in worship my left ear started to burn as if it was resting on the fiery heart of God Himself. It was not painful but rather soothing, and quite supernatural, as I could feel the warmth all around my ear. Somehow I found myself praising God through the aisle while going to the back of the sanctuary. It was there that Prophetess Agnes met me and began to pray for me.

In the midst of her prayer another crescendo of worship like a ten foot wave crashed in upon the room, and it was so voluminous that I had to sit down. She sat next to me, and there I described to her what I was feeling in respect to my ear being on fire. God then revealed to her that it was His fire touching my life as the coals did Isaiah in chapter six of his narrative. She began to prophesy about the call upon my life and the future purposes of God that were going to unfold as He set me apart for His service. From that day the trajectory of my life changed, and I held close to the mentorship of this amazing woman of God. Her affirmation and guidance was constant from that moment back in 1999, and her support remained resolute throughout my journey. Upon leaving to study for three years at the Christian International School of Theology in Florida, I made a promise before the Lord that my first book would be dedicated to her honor. Well, it is almost twenty years to the date of my promise, and here I am now humbly afforded the opportunity to fulfill my vow before the Lord.

I would also like to give God thanks for my wife, Tao Howard. She is the love of my life, my greatest intercessor outside of Christ, and a constant support. Without her I would have never been afforded the time to write and release this book for you. Her career skills in editing, design, illustration, and publication have made this book a reality. She is just super amazing, and I thank God for her beauty that is not just external, but very much internal. She is my gem and the apple of my eye. Thank you, Baby, for all you do!

Thanks to my three boys as well, Isaiah, Seraph and Jayden, who kept asking me every week about this book and kept me on my toes to reach every deadline. You guys are not just my sons but my brothers in the Lord, and you hold me to account and bring out the best in me. I am blessed to have been gifted the opportunity to steward your journey here on earth.

I would also like to acknowledge my parents. My mom, Millicent Howard, and my dad, George Franklyn Howard. When I decided to switch my career path from engineering to theology, they never flinched or questioned my decision, but supported me all the way. My mom later allowed me to know that upon my birth she had prayed a prayer of dedication for me unto the Lord, much like how Hannah did for Samuel. Thank God for praying parents! They have been a constant source of encouragement and strength to me over the years. Staying in the family, I want to also acknowledge my many aunts and uncles, especially Uncle Emmerson, my late Uncle Edgar, and my Uncle John. They have all encouraged me in my journey and offered key support along the way. On my trips to the United Kingdom, Uncle Edgar would always have a new *Scofield Study Bible* ready to gift to me. May he continue to rest in the arms of Christ.

Thanks as well to all my spiritual mentors around the globe who have encouraged me through the years. Dr. Bill Hamon, Prophet Bill Lackie (Papa Bill), Apostle Walter Boston Jr., Apostle Gale Sheehan, Prophet

Jimmy Kellett, Apostle Michael Scantlebury, Apostles Tom and Jane Hamon, Apostle Sandra Holford, Dr. Susan Slusher, Pastors David and Janis Betzer, and Apostles Jay and Jennifer McKesey. Most of all my spiritual father, Apostle Stephen Holford, who has been constant through my journey, believed in the grace of God upon my life, and has always provided a platform for my personal development. Love you, Dad!

Thank you as well to the first prophetic company that I had the opportunity to raise up back in 2007 at the launch of our local equipping center. I cannot list all of your names here, but I still have your picture framed in my office. You are the first-fruit of my prophetic equipping journey, and I am thankful that all of you are walking in your call, impacting lives, and also equipping the saints in their prophetic destiny across the world. Your yes to Jesus has made my heart full, and I am extremely thankful for you and the many that have come after you.

I finally want to thank my Awake The Flame family, leaders and global partners. Thank you for believing in the vision God has put in our hearts, serving with us in the mission, and for consistently encouraging us in the work. You are such an amazing family, and I am thankful that we have the opportunity to run together in service to God and His heart for His people. Let's continue to awaken a passion for Jesus in the nations of the earth. Love you all immensely!

Table of Contents

Foreword

The subject of prophecy has always been a very intriguing one. When we look at the Bible we see prophecy occurring from Genesis to Revelation, given by different people on different occasions. God chose men and women and entrusted the responsibility to them to be His mouthpiece in the earth, and to accurately declare what He had spoken to them. The first recorded prophecy in the Bible was given by God Himself in Genesis 3:15 where the He said to the serpent:

> "And I will put enmity between you and the woman, and between your seed and her Seed; He shall bruise your head, And you shall bruise His heel."

This was in reference to the Messiah who would come to earth and die to redeem mankind. God prophesied that Jesus would crush the power of the enemy and in the process, He would be wounded (temporarily). The ultimate fulfillment of this prophecy took place on the cross. It is no coincidence that God was the first to prophesy because He is the source of prophecy. He speaks and man echoes His voice.

Since the events in the Garden of Eden, God has raised up men and women to speak on His behalf: people like Abraham, whom the Lord called a prophet, Moses, Miriam, Samuel, Huldah, Deborah, Elijah, Isaiah,

Daniel, Peter, Paul, John, just to name a few. Each spoke as moved by the Spirit of God. They were God's mouthpiece in the earth. These men and women spoke with conviction, confidence and clarity as they declared the Lord's message. That is prophecy.

I have noticed that in the Old Testament the ministry of prophets was focused on the nation of Israel, political and spiritual leaders, and to various individuals, while in the Early Church prophets ministered to political leaders, spiritual leaders, unsaved people, and the Church. The general body of believers was encouraged to prophesy, however their ministry was limited to edification, exhortation and comfort. Today some people call them *prophesiers* or *prophetic ministers*.

There are a few criteria for the saints who prophesy:

- They should know the Lord
- They should continue to grow in Him
- They must hear the voice of the Lord
- They should speak only what He wants them to say
- They should be led by the Spirit of God

That is what this book, *Spring Up O Well* will do for you. It will train, prepare, agitate and then release you to speak forth with conviction, confidence and clarity, what the Spirit of the Lord reveals to you. Get ready for the journey of your life!

I have known Dwayne Howard for twenty-two years in various capacities—as his pastor, a family friend, as his mentor and spiritual father. After attending Bible School, he became youth minister and then some years later I had the privilege of ordaining him as a prophet and elder of New Dimensions Ministries. We have taught the prophetic class together in our equipping centre, traveled in ministry together and prophesied together. Dwayne is a profound teacher of the word and an accurate prophet who has a passion for Christ. He has spent months preparing this book and many of the concepts, protocols and instructions are from his own experience and discipline.

This book has been written as a teaching guide to educate you in the prophetic. It will help you understand what prophecy is all about, how to hear the voice of God and how to accurately speak the mind and purposes of God. It will agitate you, excite you and at the same time help you to competently impact the lives of others for Jesus through prophecy.

Apostle Stephen Holford
Senior Minister, New Dimensions Ministries, Barbados

Introduction

In an hour where powerless discipleship is celebrated and has become the comfort food of much of Christendom, *Spring Up O Well* was created as a catalyst for those who truly hunger to walk as Jesus walked, seeing greater manifestations of His Presence and power in impacting and serving the lives of others. For those who know with certainty that they were made for more than what they are currently experiencing in their walk with the Lord, this is your time. This book will agitate you to rise up from your comfort zone, embrace God's fullness for your life, and fulfill your calling. The content is biblically comprehensive, yet practical and interactive. As Christ's ambassador, you will specifically be empowered to function in your spiritual gifts, especially that of prophecy, as it is one of the many gifts that we are all invited to participate in by the Lord, even though we may all do so with different measure as Apostle Paul told the Roman church (Romans 12:6). You will learn that these gifts given by Holy Spirit are not just a means unto themselves, but a means to the end goal of releasing tangible encounter with Jesus in the lives of others, winning souls for His Kingdom, and ultimately glorifying God the Father. By no means are they graced to us for the glorifying of the practitioner, but as the same Apostle trumpeted to a stumbling Corinthian Church, their manifestation through our lives is for the profit of all people (1 Corinthians 12:7). The word profit here is also expressed as the means of making others' lives better and giving them an advantage, and what better advantage can we give than that which is rooted in Christ! As we rise to serve His purpose, we will rise to greater service in the lives of others. This holy responsibility of releasing God's gifts is not to be done recklessly or in ignorance of His instruction, lest we end up as those who are told, "Depart from Me, I know you not!" This is why within the pages of *Spring Up O Well* you will be discipled to function in the spirit of Christ, effervescing His fragrance and laboring with great effect for His glory in your everyday life. Not only will you be informed, but you will be activated—each chapter culminates with interactive faith steps and instructions to stir up the gift of God. This will aid you in stepping out of your comfort zone.

In the midst of being empowered, you will also be equipped with a biblical understanding of how prophetic promises come from the realm of articulation to actualization—from that which is spoken over you to that which springs up right before your eyes! God is not the author of confusion, and the biblical guidance and practical methodology offered here will get you on your way to walking in fulfillment. I am so excited for you, and I cannot wait to hear the many stories that will come from your life as you arise and shine for the glory of God! As you commence your journey through *Spring Up O Well* and commit to growing in Christ, feel free to email me at dwayne@awaketheflame.com, telling me of the great exploits that you have done in service of others, all for His glory and His fame. My heart waits with great expectation!

Yours In Christ,

Dwayne O. Howard

CHAPTER ONE

Embodying The Message Of The Sender

Intimacy and Prophecy Touching Humanity

"And he who sees Me sees Him who sent Me."
John 12:45 (NKJV)

Growing in God's prophetic purpose for your life is an incredible journey. He desires to bring you and me into so many depths of revelation concerning His heart and purpose, that I believe we have only just scratched the surface. In John 5:35, Jesus spoke concerning the ministry of John the Baptist and its impact. He said that John was a burning and shining lamp—one who fulfilled his call with spiritual fervency, allowing nothing to get in the way. He bore witness to the Light (John 1:6-8), released revival in the wilderness (Mark 1:4-5), and was feared by kings (Mark 6:20). John embodied the message that he was sent to deliver to such a degree, that those who heard it thought he was the 'Sender' himself (Luke 3:15). Following His remarks concerning John, Jesus goes on to make an interesting statement concerning those who preside in the Kingdom. In Matthew 11:11-12, He says that even the least in the Kingdom of Heaven is greater than he (he being John). Friends, this is not just a compliment given to every believer who accepts Jesus Christ as Lord and Savior, neither is it just an automatic designation as some may think. Rather, it is a measuring rod that should be used to evaluate our spiritual fervency and devotion. It not only paints for us a picture of God's expectation for everyone born in the Kingdom, but it indicates that there is grace given to meet and surpass that fervent standard set by John. Let's look at that scripture in Matthew a bit closer. Matthew 11:11-12 says:

> "Assuredly, I say to you, among those born of women there has not risen one greater than John the Baptist, but he who is least in the kingdom of heaven is greater than he. And from the days of John the Baptist until now the kingdom of heaven suffers violence, and the violent take it by force."

We have only just scratched the surface of what it means to be prophetic.

The context of Christ's words here do not indicate that the Kingdom of Heaven suffers violence namely from its enemies, but that the kingdom of heaven is entered into by force. *Thayer's Greek-English Lexicon of the New Testament* interprets this text as meaning that a share in the heavenly kingdom is sought for with the most ardent zeal and intense exertion. He who possesses a share possesses the profits provided by that very same kingdom. These are benefits that overtake the initial and continuing investments made within that kingdom by a person. What does this mean for us? It means that to receive the full benefits of the Kingdom of God we have to be spiritually fervent and press in for our share. God has done His part and given us access as joint heirs with Christ (Romans 8:17), but we have to do ours in the grace provided in order to experience the fullness of the glorious riches that reside in Christ, and all He purchased for us to be partakers of (Ephesians 1:18). He wants His glory to effervesce mightily from our lives, but we can't take His enabling grace in vain (2 Corinthians 6:1). May desire rise in our hearts for more! Clearly, John was a fervent vessel. He provided a good example of that spiritual violence, as Jesus could refer to John as one who had indeed pressed in and the greatest amongst those that had come before Him.

But now Jesus looks to us and says, "This is what a believer in my kingdom looks like, and furthermore, I want you to understand that John's example is minimum wage! Believers coming afterwards will be far more fiery than him."

John's example is minimum wage.

Beloved, this is an incredible statement! In our prophetic journey, we are called to greater things as compared to John's prophetic journey. Now did John spark a revival? **Yes!** Did John embody the message to the point that he was mistaken for the Sender? **Yes!** Did John's life and message pierce hearts and create genuine change? **Yes!** Did it initiate a move of sincere repentance? **Yes!** Did it shake a nation and those who dwelt in governmental and marketplace arenas? **Most definitely!** Now ask yourself this question, **"Does your life and message have the same effect?"**

Are you doing greater works?

Let's see what else Jesus has to say on this topic. In John 14:12, Jesus makes a profound statement. He says that believers in Him will do even greater works than He did. Now one argument states that Jesus's meaning was quantitive as referring to a mass of people doing more than He did. This argument seeks to make sense of Jesus' statement of doing greater works by measuring the Church's accumulated works against His while here on earth. The idea of one man doing greater works than Christ seems absurd to some and almost abominable to others. However, if we run with this interpretation we will miss what Jesus truly meant. Let's read this scripture from the *The Zondervan Parallel New Testament in Greek and English* to gain a clearer understanding of what Jesus was saying.

> "I tell you the one believing in me, the work that I do that one will do, and greater than these he will do because I go to My Father."
>
> John 14:12

The greek word for *he will do* is **poieo (poy-eh'-o)**. It is used here in the third person singular form, and indicates to the reader that Jesus was not speaking of a company of people collectively doing greater works (if so, that would be in the plural form) but rather to a single individual. This highlights for us the magnitude of the call over each of our lives personally. We need to know that Jesus expects greater works to be manifested in and through us, and by the empowerment of the Holy Spirit, even greater works surpassing His during His time on earth. Now we know Scripture reminds us that a servant can never be greater than his Master, nor a messenger greater than the One who sent him (John 13:16), but in the context of the manifestation of Holy Spirit through the believer (1 Corinthians 12:7), Jesus expects greater works from His Spirit-filled followers who are empowered by His intercession as our High Priest before the Father (Hebrews 7:25). Our obedience to the calling of God has already been designated by Him to reveal greater manifestation, and Jesus is championing us toward this end! Now I must stress that we must understand we are powerless without the Holy Spirit working in and through us, so the power is not of ourselves. But Jesus still desires to release greater prophetic words, signs and wonders, healing, teachings and miracles than when He was here on earth, and He wants to do it through you and me.

"But we have this treasure in earthen vessels, that the excellence of the power may be of God and not of us."

2 Corinthians 4:7

What you behold you become

People are usually satisfied when they reach average proficiency at any skill they set out to learn. Why is this? Because most tend to settle for average, and as sociable beings we love to hang out with the crowd. If I could only play the piano as good as Jeremy, Steve or Lucy then that would be good enough. If I could possess the charisma of Jacqui, or just articulate myself as eloquently as Anthony, then others would respect me more and be impacted by the message. Does this sound familiar? Inwardly our hearts can be easily drawn to the trappings of comparison and are content to just please man or ourselves. As long as the crowd is comfortable with our accomplishment, or as long as our accomplishment provides comfort for us, settling tends to occur.

However, in Philippians 3:14 Paul makes it clear that he is pressing toward the goal for the prize of the upward call of God in Christ Jesus. What does this statement want us to pay attention to? I would say two things specifically—Paul's face and focus. Like Paul, our face must be set in the right direction, for where your eyes go your heart and your feet will be sure to follow. His face was set upon the glorious riches of God revealed in Christ Jesus, and not upon other so-called glorious yet worldly trappings. This was the Apostle's ultimate prize, and the only one worth living for. However, one can have his face set in a particular direction yet have a distracted mind. How often are we caught staring into the eyes of someone as they converse with us yet our minds begin to wander. Paul emphasized he was not just looking in this direction but he was administering effort to stay engaged. His statement "press toward the goal" reveals that intentional activity is being employed to stay focused. The very word press in the greek means to chase, to hunt after, to set goals, and to go after something with a deep sense

He was focused and not phased! of purpose. It's not just a pie in the sky aspiration for him, but something he has determined to be deeply engaged in. He was focused and not phased! Paul was after God's highest for his life. This too, must be our desire. God's Highest! Nothing less. Our comparison should not be against others, but our heart's attention should be toward Christ and being all He has called us to be. Especially in an age of social media and being bombarded with constant agendas that seek to define accomplishment and success, we can be most vulnerable to ungodly comparison and missing God's path when we don't invest more attention towards His Presence and purpose. With all the screens we see throughout our day, this crafty world system has ample access to program and manipulate your focus, so be sure to set goals to attend to what really matters, because something else surely will. Again, where your eyes go your heart and feet will surely follow, and what you behold you will ultimately become.

"But we all, with unveiled face, beholding as in a mirror the glory of the Lord, are being transformed into the same image from glory to glory, just as by the Spirit of the Lord."

2 Corinthians 3:18

Are you a prophetic postman?

As you reorder and rightly align your heart to prioritize Him, you will quickly realize much will be added to your arsenal in respect to purpose. Many read the words of Jesus in Matthew 6:33 and think of only receiving natural provision for putting the things of the Kingdom first, but I believe spiritual equipping comes with the package. This is that which comes from the Holy Spirit in order to best serve the purpose to which you are called. These include both impartation of the charismatic gifts (1 Corinthians 12:7-10) and the cultivation of the character fruit of the Holy Spirit (Galatians 5:22-23). Some argue that they are for character and not the charismatic gifts, and this has often been due to trauma that came from the misuse of the gifts by certain individuals. However, like the growth of a tree you can have roots growing down deep and simultaneously have a trunk that grows up high with branches that stretch out wide. Both dynamics can be realized at the same time and we must go after the fullness of what God has purchased for us through all Jesus has done. This is Holy Spirit's portion for you. He who has come to lead you into all truth (John 16:13), will take the deep things of God and reveal them to your spirit (1 Corinthians 2:10-12), empowering you with greater understanding of your ambassadorial role in the Kingdom (2 Corinthians 5:20).

Interestingly, of all these great gifts you will receive there is one that you are encouraged to covet, and that is the gift of prophecy (1 Corinthians 14:39). Why you may ask? This is because it enables you to release God's mind and heart for the encouragement, edification and comfort of others (1 Corinthians 14:3). It is an amazing building tool that releases light into darkness, and brings clarity where there is confusion! It also causes the unbeliever who encounters an accurate demonstration of the gift to know that the God you serve is real and not fictitious, releasing deep conviction that can often result in conversion (1 Corinthians 14:24-25). No wonder Jesus said that His sheep hear His voice (John 10:27), as it is so necessary for our own personal walk of intimacy with God in navigating life, as well as releasing His impact to a lost world. Now if you want to go further into the foundational dynamics of the gift of prophecy, having a thorough biblical understanding of its function in the Body of Christ today, I recommend our eCourse called *Competent To Prophesy*. However, I want to challenge those who have already embraced the gift to go a step further.

As I stated earlier, sometimes we get comfortable with a basic level of proficiency and a jack of all trades attitude, and we don't go onward to the next level in our growth process. When it comes to the prophetic gift, I call this becoming a prophetic postman. So are you functioning as a prophetic postman in your prophetic proficiency? You may be scratching your head and wondering what in the world I am talking about, so let me quickly explain. A postman is one who receives the message from the sender and quickly goes his way to deliver it. From the look of the envelope, the postman can determine the company that sent it as well as the nature of its contents, but he or she has no idea concerning the details of the message.

The postman is satisfied to just deliver the message and do his job. There may be a few hellos shared and for some, gifts of appreciation from the receiver at special occasions around the year. However, the postman tends to have little to no attachment to the person receiving the message or the person sending it. Usually someone who has basic proficiency in the prophetic operates at this level. They receive a word, possess a general idea concerning the nature of the word, can give a few details surrounding the circumstance but that is about it. They can communicate the word from a general perspective which can surely bring a measure of encouragement, consolation and comfort, but not always transformation. Let me give an example below:

"A priest and a rabbi walk into a bar..." Wait a minute...wrong story, let's get serious here...

Marie and Francia

Marie has been challenging herself to step out and grow in her prophetic gift. Last spring, she even took up a Bible School elective course on the prophetic called *Competent To Prophesy*, and received a thorough understanding of the gift of prophecy and how God could use her in this regard to impact lives. Remembering Paul's exhortation to the Corinthians to earnestly desire to prophesy (1 Corinthians 14:39), and the principles of receiving spiritual things according to Mark 11:24 (possess earnest desire, contend in prayer, believe that you have received, walk it out by faith), Marie makes up in her mind that today is the day to step out in faith! She had been praying for a work colleague for over a month that God put on her heart, and felt several impressions from God to share with her. Many days she had hesitated, but not today. Today she was going to step out and share!

"Hey Francia, how are you doing today?" Marie uttered. An unusual nervousness momentarily cracked her chirpy tone.

Francia turned around to see the voice calling her name, and realized it was Marie from the front office. Besides passing her work room each morning, she only saw Marie at lunch time as colleagues gathered together around midday to munch and mingle. Francia always was curious of Marie. There was just something unique about her—besides her fluorescent wardrobe choices. She said enough to engage others while everyone carried on in the lunch room, but just little enough to create a mystery about her. Francia responded.

"Hey Marie, how's it going with you? Besides the infernal heat today in this office, I'm doing fine. Seems like the air-conditioning is broken again and hell has paid us a visit, right?"

Marie chuckled at the comment and this afforded her temporary relief from the racking of her nerves; however she quickly spoke up. "Tell me about it! It definitely is hot today but I passed the guys working on it on my way over so hopefully it will be back up soon. At least that was the promise when I asked what was going on."

Grabbing her lunch from the fridge, Francia replied, "Well, let's just keep our fingers crossed! I'd hate to have to endure this for the next three hours." Marie nodded in agreement while grabbing her lunch as well, and they both sat at the nearest table, one which accommodated just the two of them. It was round, made of glass and carried a vase in the center with faux sunflowers. As they sat, Francia chirped on about the need to replace them with the real deal. She didn't too much like the heat of the outdoors, but she sure did appreciate real flowers, by her carrying on. Meanwhile, Marie began to unwrap her sandwich while thinking that maybe today wasn't the best day to share her prophetic thoughts with Francia. After all, the heat had most in the room quite miserable and antsy, plus her commentary on the sunflowers wasn't quite the red carpet to the conversation she desired to have. Upon this thought came a swift but gentle prompting, and a still small voice whispered to Marie, "Don't miss the moment." This impression from the Spirit of God stirred courage in her heart, and after munching on her first bite she lifted her head and told Francia that she had something on her heart that she'd like to share.

Francia, who by now was chewing, was a bit surprised by the word "heart", and sprung up with eager inquisitiveness. "Go ahead Marie, I always knew there was more to you than meets the eye. I'd love to hear what's on your heart!" Marie gathered her courage, and though she thought for a moment that her train of thought had left the station and forgotten her, she caught herself, remembered the word and began to share.

"Francia, sometimes when I pray for others God shares things with me that He would like them to know. As I was praying for you, I heard Him say these things concerning you. He said to tell you that He is about to open the windows of heaven over your life and strengthen you. Many blessings will come your way, and certain dreams you have had in the past will come to pass. Your family will be blessed. You wouldn't call yourself a devoted believer per se but God knows that you have also been praying for a family member. You've been reaching out for strength to Him for that one. I sense that He would like you to know that healing is coming for that family member. He is watching over His promises concerning you. I hope this blesses you, Francia."

Francia stared Marie in the eyes, hers now glassy with hesitant tears. The atmosphere at the table had changed, and what was once an inquisitiveness about Marie became an inquisitiveness about how she could have known the things she shared.

Meanwhile, Marie felt relieved...yet a bit anxious. She waited with bated breath to hear what Francia would say. At the same time, she thought to herself whether she should have been more specific, or if what was shared was enough.

Now some of you may say that the prophetic impression shared above seems like an excellent word, full of power and hope. Indeed it is to some degree, however this only scratches the surface of what God would have us to say when we prophetically share. His desire goes beyond us giving a general understanding of what He is saying, but rather a personal and specific one that unveils the secrets of the heart and stirs worship unto Himself (1 Corinthians 14:24-25). Like John the Baptist, His desire is for us to be the very embodiment of that message, communicating the feelings of His heart and releasing the very essence of His power through the spoken word. To be in touch with man yet at home in God, is the posture of potent prophetic ministry. As suggested in this statement, such mature release comes through growing in intimacy with God, increasing in heartfelt compassion for others and a lifestyle of intercession. At this level, when the prophetic word has been released that person leaves transformed, knowing that they have indeed encountered Jesus and not just a messenger alone. Let's listen to Marie again as she now shares all of the word she received to Francia in full detail.

> **To be in touch with man yet at home in God, is the posture of potent prophetic ministry.**

"Francia, sometimes when I pray for others God shares things with me that He would like them to know. As I was praying for you, the Lord said to tell you that He has seen your labor of love and commitment here in this workplace, and how you've striven to balance it with your home responsibilities and family. There are times where you beat yourself

up because you think you've dropped the ball trying to do it all, and with that you even cry out in secret saying 'God, why can't my children have a mother that is better than me?' However He wants you to know you are the woman for the job and none could do it better. He says to let you know that He is proud of you and all of your effort expended. You couldn't have known that you'd have to do it all alone when that once special person walked out through the door, but He says that He wants you to know that He will never walk out on you. He says, 'I am with you Francia, and I will never leave you nor forsake you, but will be by your side to strengthen and assist you as you walk this out.' Yes support grew thin and the walls were caving in, but yet you chose to endure, you chose to take a stand, and you were able to do this because I was holding you with My Hand. And as I am with you, so shall I be with your children.

*Francia you have often wondered if they **will see their dreams fulfilled**, or if their capacity for opportunity will be stunted by the next bill. Your dreams are intertwined with theirs indeed, and do know that God says He is with them to see them succeed. Yet you ask, 'Lord, why didn't my family believe me, why did they just blame me?' And He says, 'Daughter, rest and know that your prayer avails much." For those who have spoken ill of you, **they too will come to know** and like Joseph you will pave the way for them through your intercession so that they may grow. As for you though, God says continue to trust in Him. He also knows this **infirmity of cancer** has manifested not once but twice upon your dear friend, a friend that has been more like family to you in recent times. You've been anxious about just the thought of losing her. However He says it will not have her. Only trust in Him, for **her deliverance comes quickly**. The hour of her healing is indeed near. Be strengthened Francia, God loves you and He is with you and those you love."*

Made for more than you can imagine

I want you to notice that all of the areas mentioned in the initial prophetic word are highlighted and mentioned in this one. However, one can sense that there is a greater release of compassion from the Lord with more specifics and anointing released to break the yokes of despair and disillusionment over Francia. As you read, you can imagine Marie, the messenger, communicating not just the words that God gave, but the mood (emotion) He intended for it. Her voice carries anointed inflection that has been carved out of time spent in hearing God's heart. This time spent before the Lord and crying out for her friend has softened her heart in such a way that she has yielded and become a greater embodiment of the message, and this is what God is calling us to—not to be another prophetic postman just showing up to do our job, but to be potent prophetic messengers that effervesce His abundant life.

Like Jesus, we will be able to say that he who sees me, sees Him who sent me (John 12:45), and those who receive from us will know that they have not received from man, but from God through a yielded vessel. This is where the intersection of intimacy and prophecy truly touches humanity. Some have used and obsessed over the prophetic as a tool to elevate selfish ideals, but God's intention is to elevate His Purpose and Presence that hearts can be transformed for His glory. Let us hunger to have our share in the right company.

This hunger for more starts with the understanding that God has created you to flow in this capacity. We have made this clear for you by journeying through the words of Jesus concerning John the Baptist and also Himself in the commencement of this chapter, and as we move on we will discuss a life lived in this reality.

> **Not just the words that God gave, but the mood He intended for it.**

Now Marie prepared her heart for a colleague, but what about circumstances where we are engaging others for the first time. How do we ready our hearts to flow and bestow the goodness of God in and out of season, to be a witness in every context and at every time? How do we maximize the moment and live as a well that never runs dry, springing up as a blessing for those we engage along the way? Let's follow on to the next chapter as the journey continues.

Go Deeper

List three ways you will challenge
yourself to grow.

1.

2.

3.

CHAPTER TWO

Naturally Supernatural

Practical Christianity at its Best

"He who says he abides in Him ought himself
also to walk just as He walked."
1 John 2:6 (NKJV)

Authentic demonstration

What we were robbed of because of the sin of the first man Adam, was restored because of the sacrifice of the God Man, Jesus Christ (Romans 5:17). As joint heirs, our call to walk as revealers of God's glory in the earth has been authenticated by Jesus Himself, through obedience to the will of the Father. Through Him we receive God's abundant provision of grace that enables us to reign in life, and this reign is not selfish, but incredibly generous in its assignment to glorify God. Notice the last five words of that last sentence. Read them again, and read them aloud! This is where simplicity meets the profound. It is simple to us in that it is freely given in Christ, but it is profound in that it is accessed and manifested accurately only through vessels who care not for personal gratification or glory. As our key scripture implies (1 John 2:6), it is the one who refuses to walk by means of his own way, but rather gives preference to His way, walking as He walked. These are the true disciples of Christ that not only articulate, but demonstrate. These are the ones that understand that if we are to fully hone the supernatural walk that is afforded in Him, an investment of "not my will, but Yours be done" must be heavily considered. These are the ones who turn their backs on the realm of an empty profession, and choose to walk in the realm of demonstration. They don't merely have a profession of faith, but a progression of faith!

> "We are bound to thank God always for you, brethren, as it is fitting, because your faith grows exceedingly, and the love of every one of you all abounds toward each other."
>
> 2 Thessalonians 1:3

They don't merely have a profession of faith, but a progression of faith!

Now anyone can walk in the dynamics of a gifting. In fact, all nine gifts of the Spirit (1 Corinthians 12:6-10) can be functioned in yet the person utilizing the gift can still miss the mark (1 Corinthians 13:1-3). You might be amazed to discover that you can live quite contrary to the character of Christ yet still demonstrate supernaturally, for it is a gift accessed by faith (Romans 12:6, Ephesians 2:8). The Word of God allows us to know that He permits this so to test and reveal the hearts of His people (Deuteronomy 13:3). God distinctly says here in Deuteronomy through Moses to not listen to such a person, yet even in our age some will ignore telling signs of corruption in another just to receive some blessing from their gift. There are some as well who will function in a gift while practicing willful and blatant corruption, and find comfort in the fact that the gift is still accurate. You must understand that the gift does not validate your identity, but is separate from it. Just as possessing a toolkit doesn't make one a mechanic, flowing in a spiritual gift cannot verify one's accuracy of heart. You may sound dazzling to the ears of men, but dissonant to the ears of God. This is why we must always have first things first (Revelation 2:4), and to do so one must embark on three practical examinations to ensure a proper overhaul of motive, mindset and ministry. Let's examine these below and ask ourselves some questions along the way.

My Motive

Your motive is deeply connected to what the Bible refers to as your heart. It speaks to your reason for doing something (Matthew 12:34), is the revealer of hidden inner desire (Proverbs 23:7), and can be seen as the thing that drives you (Proverbs 19:21). Honestly answering these questions below will help you navigate your motivation. Ask Holy Spirit to lead you to the discovery of truth in this regard before commencing (John 16:13).

Ask yourself:

1. Why do I want to see God's glory manifest through my life? Pray and ask Holy Spirit right now to help you examine your motivation (the thing that truly drives you).
2. Have my conversations been about His plans recently, or my own? Pray and ask Holy Spirit right now to help you examine your mouth (the content and focus of your words).
3. Do I care more about my own reputation than reverencing Him with my life? Pray and ask Holy Spirit right now to help you examine your metrics (Is it about self preservation or God's exaltation?).
4. Do I intentionally invite Him into my decisions, to interrupt, suspend or give allowance? Pray and ask Holy Spirit right now to

help you examine your methods (Are they God inclusive, instructed or directed?).

By working through these questions you are navigating the inner corridors of your heart, and it is upon that walk that you will truly discover what doors you have kept locked from Him, and what doors you have opened to Him. Obviously nothing is hidden from His eyes, but even so He will not force you to yield. It has to be a surrender of one's will with a desire for the Holy Spirit to fully consume and fill. The last question is of particular interest, because it speaks to a daily yielding to God in all things. Whether that means on your commute to work, while swiping through social media or shopping at the supermarket, room for the plans of the Lord to supersede your own must be afforded.

I remember reclining in my couch after a long day of work, and casually scrolling through Twitter as I waited for a basketball game to commence on cable TV. I would usually catch up on basketball scores and the hype accounts of those who support my team, but this time as I was scrolling something caught my eye. There was a tweet released from a woman who couldn't decide if to have an abortion due to the fact that she didn't want her paramour to be the father of her first child. Now on Twitter you can come across statements like this everyday, and I really just wanted to relax from a long day and not have to deal with the problems of the world. However, God interrupted my scrolling and my spirit wouldn't settle until I went back to the conversation. He wanted me to be gripped just as He was for this young lady, and so I stayed there and began to pray for her decision, and for conviction to rest on her heart. I also felt His leading to offer a counter-culture response in wisdom to the conversation that was now laden with responses saying to "kill that thing". All of this while just trying to relax and watch some basketball. Yet if my life is not my own, my willingness to advance His purposes will always be greater than my own.

It is in these moments that our motivation is tested. Not necessarily our motivation for what we choose to do, but our motivation for who we choose to be. Will I identify with the things that bring Him glory, or will I identify with bringing the "Idol of Me" glory? I make the following sentiment a daily reminder that I regurgitate.

It always makes sense to walk as He walked!
For through the eyes of eternity, anything less would
be as if you had never walked at all.

In the film *Braveheart*, the valiant William Wallace now imprisoned and ready for death, looks into the eyes of the beautiful Princess Isabelle who for love desired that he recant his stand and preserve his own life. He tells her these memorable words: "Every man dies, but not every man truly lives!" Beloved, as a child of God called to great things in God, surrender your motivation and truly live a life worthy of the sacrifice of the Lamb.

My Mindset

The mind is the seedbed for thoughts, and it is these thoughts that either produce life or produce death. Over and over in the word of God we are compelled to renew our minds, for our minds are either being conformed or transformed (Romans 12:2). Such thoughts come from three realms:

1. The Mind of Man (Soulish)
2. The Mind of Christ (Spiritual)
3. The Mind of The Deceiver (Satanic)

In order to have a healthy mindset that enforces fruitfulness in your walk, God grants us an amazing piece of equipment called the helmet of salvation. The Apostle Paul refers to it in his letter to the Ephesians (6:17), however he elaborates on it as he writes to the Thessalonians, a people who were under severe pressure and persecution (1 Thessalonians

1:6). Here he calls the helmet we are called to put on *the hope of salvation* (1 Thessalonians 5:8). Now this hope we speak of is not worldly hope as the greeks defined it—one that shifts between whether something good is going to happen or something bad. No, not at all! Rather, biblical hope is defined as a steady expectation that is founded and based on the trustworthiness of God to keep His promises. It is a confident expectancy in God, and this confidence guards your mind, keeps your mind, and feeds your mind. This hope in your mind is an essential component of your salvation experience and walk with God. If you do not have hope in the benefits and empowerment that salvation affords, then you won't cultivate the drive necessary for authentic demonstration.

Furthermore, you must be intentional about taking hold of it, for the word Paul used for take in Ephesians 6:17 (take the helmet) means to choose to receive and welcome. You must choose to receive biblical hope and welcome it into your heart daily. This is how you protect your mind in the warfare, because your enemy is definitely going to be intentional about bombarding your mind with lies. Despite the headlines of varying reports filling the airwaves, you must engage a constant flow of God's Word wave! This is His voice speaking to you the words that come alive as you abide in The Word.

Your desire for bringing Him glory through your life is reflected in part by your pursuit of His promises in Christ Jesus. If you don't know what those promises are and what you have been granted as a new creation in Christ Jesus (2 Corinthians 5:17), then you will easily fold under pressure because another voice would have filled the vacuum. Usually this is a voice of fear, guilt or intimidation. You see, in war there is no territory that resides unconquered. The mind of man is either being transformed by the truth of God's promises, or being conformed to the lies of the deceiver. This is why it is critical for you to know God's prophetic promises, and war with them in your life (1 Timothy 1:18). Answering these questions below will help you to evaluate if you're wearing your helmet of hope.

Ask yourself:

1. Do I struggle with the thought that God won't come through for me like how He has come through for others?
2. Do I believe that I have messed up so badly that I have forfeited God's best for my life?
3. Do I have an expectation that if something goes well in my life, something will happen soon after that goes badly?
4. Have I ever thought that God has shortchanged me?
5. I feel as though God has failed me before, and He may do it again. Can I open my heart to that type of disappointment again?

In considering these questions, the pricking you may have felt in your heart is an indicator that you have taken damage to the head already in the battle. Healing is therefore the next step, and that means walking back through that disappointment audibly with God, expressing with full openness your pain, and then waiting on Him to speak to your heart in His Presence. This is where you choose to worship like Job in the midst of your circumstance (Job 1:21), gazing into His Word despite, and deliberately taking the time to remedy your soul. Investing in good christian counseling and deliverance may be helpful in such times as well. Know that you're not alone in this, as great biblical characters such as Asaph (as seen in Psalm 73) and Hannah (as seen in 1 Samuel 1), all suffered the same issues but found their rescue by waiting on the Lord in His Presence. As it was with them when healing came, make a promise to keep steady hope in His promises. Remember the great things He has done, and let it fuel your expectation of the great things He will do!

My Ministry

The word *ministry* literally speaks of one's service to another, and the job of aligning motive and building the proper mindset will give you a key advantage and thrust towards your step into supernatural service. Getting the heart and mind right creates great momentum, but one more ingredient will take you all the way onward into a radically supernatural life. You see, if motive is the righting of the heart, and mindset is the renewing of the mind, then ministry is the readiness of both hands and feet. Here the readiness of the hands of ministry speaks to plowing (Luke 9:62), while the readiness of the feet speaks to progressing (Ephesians 6:15).

If we are going to be fit for service (ministry) in the Kingdom according to Jesus, then we can't take our hands off the plow. In therefore considering what we must do, it is good practice to take a look at what we must not. Let's look at a character who took his hand off the plow.

Lessons from Demas

Demas had been at one time a fellow worker of the Apostle Paul (Philemon 1:24, Colossians 4:14), but along the way his life took a tragic turn. Let's look at this scripture below:

> "Be diligent to come to me quickly; for Demas has forsaken me, having loved this present world, and has departed for Thessalonica..."
>
> 2 Timothy 4:9-10

Cracking under pressure

Demas made a decision at a critical juncture to choose delighting in Satan's promises rather than God's. Paul stresses that Demas forsook him and the ministry in a time of need, because of his desire for pleasure in what the age of that time could offer. Instead of being ready for his assignment, Demas retreated from it. Somewhere along the journey, his heart succumbed to despair and his mind got topped up with deception. These infections rotted out his readiness.

The spirit of Demas

In order to fulfill your assignment, you must not allow infections caused by open wounds to fester. These open wounds will drain your drive and eclipse your energy. Prioritize healing, put on the helmet of salvation, and inspect what you expect. We must ensure our expectation is aligned with God's hope, whether granted through personal prophecy or a biblically declared reality (promise spoken by God in the Bible). False expectation will always lead to great disappointment, so test all things and hold fast to that which is good. Examine all prophetic words in light of the written Word, and ensure that your taking hold of promises written in the biblical narrative is done through Christ-centric theology (what has been afforded and made accessible to us in God through Christ by the Holy Spirit). If we fail to do this, we give opportunity for the spirit of Demas to come and unclench our hand from the plow. Don't allow despair to cause you to forget why you are here!

Inspect what you expect.

Feet readied with the gospel of peace

In Ephesians 6:15, we see that we have to shod our feet with the preparation of the gospel of peace. Paul took this imagery of feet being shod from Roman legionnaires, who wore sandal-boots (caligae) that were strong and had cords that strung up to the calf. They were heavy duty and thick soled, made from calf skin or ox hide, and used to ensure mobility, optimum grip and readiness throughout battle and long journeys. They were intricately created and hardly removed in seasons of warfare. This ensured that the soldier would always be ready for battle even in the dead of night, especially if there was a surprise attack of the enemy.

In the same manner, we need to ensure our feet are ready to advance and not trip. It means we must be strapped up, which speaks of one's preparation. You are not going to see the results that come with progression if there is poor preparation. You are not going to feel the peace of God in your assignment if there is poor preparation. You must season yourself in His Presence if you're going to be supernatural in the world's presence. A favorite preacher of mine often said this:

"Hours with God make minutes with men!" - Guillermo Maldonado

This confidence to step out and see major outpourings of God's power also starts with your management of smaller opportunities. Being faithful in the little still qualifies you into the realm of much, however you have to be faithful and make preparations to use the talent that you possess (Matthew 25:14-30). If you're letting the little opportunities pass you by—like that family member that needs to be encouraged prophetically or that neighbor that needs healing prayer, then you will struggle in unfamiliar territory. Even Jesus told his disciples to start first at Jerusalem, then Judea and Samaria, then unto the ends of the earth (Acts 1:8). The key is to progress with what you know, and God will make it grow. So why are you waiting? Let's go!

> **You must season yourself in His presence if you're going to be supernatural in the world's presence.**

Go Deeper

On a scale of 1-10 (1 being pretty poor and 10 being superb),
how would you rate the quality of your motive, your mindset
and your ministry?

Motive rating:

Mindset rating:

Ministry rating:

List three familiar people you can be faithful to step out and prophetically minister to or pray for healing with this week.

1. ____

2. ____

3. ____

CHAPTER THREE

Breakthrough Beyond Your Comfort Zone

Saying Goodbye to the Fake and Fruitless Life

"For the earnest expectation of the creation eagerly
waits for the revealing of the sons of God."
Romans 8:19 (NKJV)

Lost in wonder, love and praise

Charles Wesley, inspired by the worshiping elders and heavenly hosts in Chapter 4 of the Revelation of Jesus Christ, so poetically expressed in his hymn *Love Divine, All Loves Excelling*, that we are called as God's creation to be lost in wonder before His Glorious Person! However, one of the greatest tragedies that has occurred in the universal Church is the loss of wonder in God's Person. Our eyes have been lent to other so-called wondrous things, whether it be the latest technological advancement or the CGI engineered Hollywood spectacle, that we have settled on the hills of fascination as opposed to rising up to

29

the mountain of truly perceiving the beauty of God's Holiness (Jeremiah 50:6). His beauty no longer moves us as it does the angels, but God longs to restore our vision and capability to discover wonder in Him.

> "My people have been lost sheep. Their shepherds have led them astray;
> They have turned them away on the mountains. They have gone from
> mountain to hill; they have forgotten their resting place."
>
> Jeremiah 50:6

David, King of Israel, makes this prayer in Psalm 119:18, as he too was probably experiencing what we are at present. He says to God, "Open my eyes, that I may see wondrous things from Your law." Is there any other cry nobler or sincere as this? God, open my eyes to behold your beauty! I have been distracted and consumed with other things that have made my walk in You fake and fruitless, so now I humbly return to You. I want to be fascinated by Your splendor and overwhelmed by Your Presence, to the point that everything else simply becomes a lesser love and a shadow in the light of You. I desire that my heart would melt again as I gaze deeply into Your Word. I am desperate to see wondrous things! I want to truly witness the Light that is You.

To bear true witness of the Light

So what does regaining wonder in God's Word have to do with speaking prophetically? Beloved, it has everything to do with it. Your time spent in beholding His Beauty as revealed in the written Word will compliment your ability to communicate His Beauty via a prophetic word. This ensures your representation is authentic and anointed. The Bible says of John the Baptist that he came to bear witness of the Light (John 1:6-8), and Jesus complimented John upon his testimony of the Light, affirming that He was indeed a true witness (John 5:33,35). Now a true witness can be compared to what is known in our courts as an eye-witness. An eye-witness is one who has seen the truth first hand and there is little to no doubt concerning their testimony. They can provide convincing evidence to win a case and ensure a correct decision from the jury. In the same way, one whose eyes have been opened to discover wondrous things from God will serve at a greater depth of Presence and impact than another who is dull in vision. Just like the eye-witness, there will be greater confidence and accuracy in your prophetic utterance, and all of heaven will rally to work along with the word to see its fulfillment in the earth realm.

We see this with the prophet Elijah, a man who James of the New Testament said was a man just like us (James 5:17), yet James stresses that heaven backed his words. In the record of the Kings of Israel and Judah (1 Kings 17:1), Elijah commands the rain not to fall unless he gives the word for it to do so. Notice Elijah does not say unless God gives the word, but unless he gives the word. Why was he so bold to make such a declaration? The clue to discovering the source of his confidence is found in what is said when he is introduced at the beginning of the chapter. He is declared as one who came from standing before the Presence of God. This is all we know of Elijah's history, and truthfully, all we need to know. His life was a sign and a wonder because he was lost in the well of wonder, that is, the wellspring of God's Presence! Heaven backed up his words because he was soaked in the Presence of the One who is The Word!

Can your prophetic utterance be trusted?

Not only Elijah, but the prophetic utterances of others were held in high regard because of their soaking in the counsel of the Wonderful Counselor (Isaiah 9:6). We see this example in the life of Daniel (Daniel 9:1-2), who was able to war for his people's freedom with the prophetic words of the late prophet Jeremiah (Jeremiah 25:1-11, 29:1-10). Daniel understood that Israel was locked into 70 years of desolation and Babylonian servitude by studying the prophecy, and was able to then pray for His people's release as these years were coming to an end. The question for us who dwell in a better covenant than Elijah, Daniel and Jeremiah is this, can your prophetic utterance be trusted to this measure? Can the word that leaves your lips carry potency that will set captives free and give strategy to others that they may know how to wage a good warfare?

Over the years, I have humbly been afforded the opportunity to serve many pastoral leaders, governmental officials (saved and unsaved), business leaders and the everyday believer, in helping them discern spiritual enigmas, dreams and walking out their prophetic promises. Even as I am writing this chapter, I had to take a break to respond to a voice-note from a close friend in ministry who contacted me several days ago for some assistance. He and his wife had the same dream on the same night, and he wanted to hear my thoughts on what that dream meant. I took several days to reply to him due to my schedule and desire to pray for them first, but when I did, his response to the interpretation I shared was this:

"All of what you said resonates, and some things you shared you could have never known. We now have the confidence to take the steps we felt that we needed to take, as we go faith first into God's next step for us."

These kinds of responses are humbling yet invigorating! It's exciting when God can take over and empower you to help someone in such a way that would be impossible in your own natural ability. Most of all, it reminds me of the need to treasure His Presence and stay lost in the wonder of His great love for us all.

"And there is no creature hidden from His sight, but all things are naked and open to the eyes of Him to whom we must give account."
Hebrews 4:13

He is gracious to never leave us in the dark, but have us walk in the light. We just have to be available because He has made Himself accessible

(Hebrews 4:16, Proverbs 8:17). Let us therefore give ourselves to standing in His Counsel, because if we don't, our prophetic counsel will fall short of aiding and serving the lives of others. As God's prophetic people, we cannot afford to live life in the comfort zone of lesser loves. This does not mean that we shouldn't have room for soul food on the plate of life. Soul foods include the natural things we enjoy or do to relax and kick back, and it is wholesome once it is done in moderation. However, when we overextend ourselves in the soul category and deny our spirit the majority of the pie, it becomes a death sentence for our spiritual fervency. The lethargy that comes after we overindulge in the natural, is the same effect that transpires in the soul when we splurge in one area and loose connection with the food that really matters (John 4:34).

In the realm of fitness, your plate has to be rounded to suit the goal you want to achieve. You may need a keto meal or a high protein plate that has less calorie inducing starches in order to accomplish proper weight loss and encourage lean muscle gains. In the same way, what we feed ourselves on consistently will determine the results we are left with in spiritual matters. Consistency is the key word here, as some have had major accomplishment in the past but now feel like they have lost their fire or spiritual fervor. Remember Jesus' words to the church of Ephesus about returning to their first love and reclaiming the fire of intimacy (Revelation 2:1-12)? We all come under the admonishment of this statement ever so often, but it is best we learn from it and stay a steady course. When we don't, we lose the transformative power that comes from beholding Him as an eye witness (2 Corinthians 3:18), and demote ourselves to case witness status (someone with a past experience). You don't want this to be your story. Those who fall into this category in the courts of men, are those who may have known the person on trial for a long time, but lack knowledge concerning their present activity as relating to the case. They can tell the court that they know this individual to be a nice person and that they are kind and would never steal, but they lack **present truth**, and thus their witness is not as convincing as the eye-witness's. Do you see the difference? We must be established in present truth (2 Peter 1:12), thus being true witnesses to the Light. **This is one of the most important steps to enhancing your prophetic delivery and experiencing breakthrough beyond your comfort zone.**

Are you a carrier?

Your growth in breaking religious norms and stepping out is truly hinged upon this journey of personal engagement and experiential knowledge of the Word Himself. Galatians 3:26 reminds us that we are sons of God through faith in Jesus Christ, and if we haven't already, we must fully embrace the significance of this word that has been declared over us. What does it mean to be a son? Well, let us first adventure into what it takes to create a son. In every pregnancy, medical research has revealed that it is the father's seed that determines the sex of the child. Within this seed, genetic information is carried in a self-replicating material called deoxyribonucleic acid (DNA). This information is decoded and referred to as our genes, which in turn determines personality traits, body formulation, and other important aspects. However, from a spiritual perspective, God our heavenly Father has given us His seed, Jesus Christ, who in his death gave birth to many other seeds (John 12:24). As the father's seed determines the sex, so in God's foreknowledge we were predetermined to be, by faith in Jesus Christ, sons of God that Jesus might be the firstborn among many brothers (Romans 8:29). In being sons, we are also joint heirs with Jesus our big brother, and that indicates that what He possesses, we too possess by right of our adoption (Romans 8:14-18). Thus as He carried authority, royalty, power and enforced kingdom legislation in the earth, so too are we called to function. As we see in our key scripture, all creation is groaning for us to take our rightful place.

So are you ready to be a carrier? A carrier of what may be your obvious question, but my inference is being a carrier of God's glory in the earth, just as your big brother Jesus was and is. Are you unleashing the treasure in your earthen vessel as He did (2 Corinthians 4:7)? Do people know that God's effervescence is present when they are in your presence? Has your spiritual DNA been unleashed? Let's go further as we believe to see these dimensions of God's glory manifest in your life!

Your Prophetic DNA

I would like to first define DNA as an acronym to represent what the Bible speaks of concerning our makeup as sons of God, and in turn, reflect upon the impact it brings to our prophetic calling. This DNA is Distinction, Nobility and Accuracy.

Distinction is defined as:
1. A difference or contrast between similar things or people
2. Excellence that sets someone or something apart from others

Distinction
Nobility
Accuracy

Genesis 1:26-28 declares that God created man in His image and in His likeness, placing authority upon him to rule, increase and subdue. As we saw in the last chapter, though this heavenly initiative was compromised with Adam, it was restored in Christ (1 Corinthians 15:22, Romans 5:14), and must be carried out by His church as we co-labor with Him (Luke 10:19). We must rule, increase and subdue the enemy and the earth for Christ (1 John 3:8, Revelations 11:15). As it corresponds to us flowing as a prophetic people who hear His Voice, we must first remember that our prophetic foundations are energized by faith which works through love (Romans 12:6, Galatians 5:6). Our prophetic release must be different from that of the ungodly because we serve the living God. They practice divination, but we function in distinction. Ours must be more than informational, as patterned by the ungodly, practitioner of dark arts who is fed by familiar spirits in the unseen realm. Rather, it must be transformational with utterances infused with the weightiness of God's measure for His Word (Psalm 29). Our function must truly reflect the reality that we are constructed in God's image and we operate in the likeness of Him, bringing deliverance, conviction, restoration and creative power to the life of the receiver (John 10:10). God's released word is a fire that consumes and a hammer that breaks the rock in pieces (Jeremiah 23:29), and as we speak for Him we should have such expectation that heaven will come, earth will be shaken, and hell will shatter. Though we know God is sovereign and determines what He releases through a vessel, He is impressed by faith and our willingness to trust Him (The Centurion of Matthew 8:5-10). We must believe, receive and release!

> **We should have such expectation that heaven will come, earth will be shaken, and hell will shatter!**

Nobility is defined as:
1. The quality of being noble in character, mind, birth or rank.
2. A group of people belonging to a noble class in a country, especially those with a hereditary or honorary title.

1 Peter 2:9 declares that we are a chosen people, a royal priesthood, a holy nation, a people belonging to God, that we may declare the praises of Him who called us out of darkness into His wonderful light. One of our greatest assets in gaining revelation from God comes from the position we hold in His heart. We are part of the royal family of God and are chosen to share in what He has revealed to us (Deuteronomy 29:29). With such access, we can probe the mind of God concerning a person we are to minister to. It's one thing to receive information from God as one listens, but it is another thing to discuss with God the different issues in

the person's life that you may sense a concern for. We will explore this further in the next chapter. Do not feel limited in your relationship with God, but know that He has given you bold entrance through the blood of His Son (2 Corinthians 3:7-18, Hebrews 4:15-16) to come before Him and inquire (Psalm 27:4, Genesis 18:20-33).

Accuracy is defined as:
1. The quality or state of being correct or precise.
2. The ability to perform a task with precision.

Hebrews 4:12 sets a standard for the Word of the Lord. It is sharper than any two-edged sword, penetrating even to dividing soul and spirit, joints and marrow; it judges the thoughts and attitudes of the heart. The author goes on in the following verse to ensure us that God is omniscient, with nothing being hidden from His sight. As we dwell in Him, the confidence of this reality empowers us. We will not be afraid to step out of the boats of comfort that we are accustomed to. Like Peter, we will step out as He calls us knowing that He cannot fail (Matthew 14:28-29). God will often challenge you to get very specific in your prophetic release, and it is at those times that our lack of faith can become so apparent. However, as you grow near to Him and utilize the access He has given you in relationship, you will find this becomes easier. Set your mind not on yourself, but upon Him as you stand in the gap for the transformation of another. Imagine that person being invigorated, secured, healed, delivered and encouraged, and you will soon see that He will do exceedingly, abundantly and above what you imagine (Ephesians 3:20).

Unleash God's potential

These three areas are realistic dimensions of our lives and should be affirmed as we press in for greater impact in our prophetic flow to others. Remember, God's goal is to transform and uplift the person to whom you will minister, so unleash your prophetic DNA and allow the Holy Spirit to have His way in and through your life. It would be a shame to depart this life and in eternity look back at what God could have done through you. Friends, let Him have His way.

Go Deeper

Read Psalm 29 and list seven attributes of God's Word.
Place the verse reference from the psalm beside each attribute.

1. ____

2. ____

3. ____

4. ____

5. ____

6. ____

7. ____

In John 21, Peter struggled to see himself as Jesus saw him, and he felt unfit for the ministry he was called to. What beliefs are making you feel unfit, and what is giving them power over you?

CHAPTER FOUR

Releasing the Spirit of Prophecy

Practical Methods that Release the Miraculous

"Worship God! For the testimony of
Jesus is the spirit of prophecy."
Revelation 19:10 (NKJV)

All is for His glory

We are often taught to study the Book of Revelation with our gaze set on eschatology (the study of the end times and the final destiny of the soul), while forgetting that it is more so about Christology (the part of theology interested with the nature and work of Jesus). It would be wise for us to remember that this prophetic book is titled, "The Revelation of Jesus Christ", The greatest asset of this prophecy isn't for the purpose of us determining ourselves to be preterist, post or pre-tribulation believers, but disciples firmly seated in the ever-increasing knowledge of Him, occupying until He comes and thus ready for His appearing. The One who stands as the Faithful Witness to the Father (Hebrews 1:1-5, Revelation 1:5), who is worthy to take the scroll and unleash His perfect wisdom and power to the ends of the earth in securing His inheritance (Revelation 5:2-7, Psalm 2:8), calls us to be found in Him as prophetic vessels whose impact is weighed not by articulation and language alone, but by an active lifestyle that testifies of Him. Let me tell you, the greatest prophetic word you will ever give is a life that truly reflects and bears witness to Christ. You have not been called to impact lives by releasing the gift of prophecy—as if it were just but a mere practice of letting words out of your mouth—but to the transformation of hearts by releasing the spirit of prophecy. This creates a precedent for the prophetic opportunity to serve others as being set on encounter with His Person and not just mere engagement with your own.

> ## Authentic prophetic ministry is all about revealing and testifying of Jesus.

We have placed emphasis on this reality in the preceding chapters, but it is always a good reminder to have our ducks in a row and priorities in check. Let us be sure to always guard our hearts so that our interest is not set in becoming skilled with a gift just as the Pharisees were skilled with the letter, but to be full of the Spirit and the power of His might! I have witnessed in my time of doing ministry some who have believed they were full of the Spirit because they were flowing in the gifts of the Spirit, yet they fell into error and some even forsook their walk with Jesus. Remember the gifts are irrevocable (Romans 11:29), and you can use them just as Saul did while walking in error (1 Samuel 19:24). This is why authentic prophetic ministry is all about revealing and testifying of Jesus, and it means that practically we must abide in Him and not forsake His nearness in the midst of being zealous about manifesting great works (Revelation 2:1-5). Remember the words of Paul to the gifted Corinthian believers:

> "And we have such trust through Christ toward God. Not that we are sufficient of ourselves to think of anything as being from ourselves, but our sufficiency is from God, who also made us sufficient as ministers of the new covenant, not of the letter but of the Spirit; for the letter kills, but the Spirit gives life."
>
> 2 Corinthians 3:4-6 (NKJV)

I have not spoken on my own

Jesus was careful with His words. In John 12:49, He makes it clear that He has not spoken on His own accord, but the Father who sent Him endowed Him with the commands of what to say and of what to speak. If our hearts are truly set on glorifying Jesus, then we must follow His example. One of the ways we can practically do so is by diligently surveying the descriptions of how the Father defines the quality and power of His Voice. At the end of the last chapter, I submitted to you an exercise of studying Psalm 29 and capturing seven attributes of His voice. I hope you explored this, because we will be doing so together shortly. However let us first look to another Psalm that David penned, describing the words of the Lord.

> "The words of the LORD are pure words, like silver tried in a furnace of earth, purified seven times."
>
> Psalm 12:6 (NKJV)

The Imrah of Yahweh

The call to prophesy (Ephesians 4:11, 1 Corinthians 14:31) is to accurately deliver the intent and mind of God to men, which to the receiver can be shrouded by ambiguity for a time (Isaiah 6:9-10), or made bare in full clarity in a moment (Jonah 3:1-5). This delivery often involves utterance. In Psalm 12:6, the Psalmist emphasizes the concept of vocal speech and utterance in correlation to the prophetic, and places further emphasis on the supreme reliability of words that flow from God. Throughout the content of this psalm however, David draws a stark contrast between the deceitfulness of the tongues of men and the faithfulness of God's words, with the crescendo of this contention being ratified in the Lord delivering His people (Psalm 12:5). Here we witness a constant theme that is repeated throughout scripture—men's helplessness in rescuing themselves but rather wrecking themselves, and God's faithfulness to stand true to Himself and deliver (2 Timothy 2:13). As David declares the mind of the Lord in Psalm 12:6, a reassurance follows revealing the trustworthiness of what God speaks. The word in the Hebrew that is used here for *words* is *imrah*, and its meaning is both familiar and special. Let's peruse the definition below.

Imrah

—utterance, speech, instruction, a promise, synonymous to the greek word *rhema*.

In Psalm 105:19, this very same word is used to identify the word of the Lord that was given to Joseph, that in turn tried him. Amongst the prophets, Isaiah also uses it to describe his prophetic proclamations (Isaiah 32:9). This gives us enough evidence to understand that what David described in our key text was reflective of the prophetic words and proclamations of God. Now let's investigate their nature as defined by him under the inspiration of the Holy Spirit.

Belonging to Yahweh

David starts the conversation by reminding us that the words (Imrah) belong to Yahweh. In essence, he is stating that they have their origin in

Him. Our desire to work alongside God as His prophetic people should always start with the foundation of sitting at His feet, choosing the better part like Mary of Bethany (Luke 10:42). Her shared story with her sister Martha is a great reminder that our service to Him must commence from the posture of worshiping, and not just working. This posture of intimacy with Him ensures we start right, and if we start right we are more than likely to finish well. God's desire is for His wisdom to spring up from the well of our hearts, but what good is a well without water friends. If we are to truly reveal the mysteries of His heart to men, then we have to abide in Him and walk in the power of His Spirit (John 15:4-6, 1 Corinthians 2:1-16).

PURE WORDS

David continues the conversation by stating that the words of Yahweh are pure words. This descriptive adjective literally means flawless or lacking impurities. The utterance that flows from God's fount is without error in space, time and eternity, and is characteristic of Him and Him alone. Now, we are not God, but we are indeed His chosen instruments (Acts 9:15 NASB), ambassadors of Christ (2 Corinthians 5:20), His temple in the earth realm (1 Corinthians 6:19), and it is His desire to reveal His Person through you and me (Matthew 5:16, Isaiah 60:1-2). However, if an instrument remains untuned then who can properly play it. If a temple remains in ruins, then who can rightly abide in it. This is why as ambassadors, we must stay in alignment with our assignment if we are going to function with Heaven's authorization. It is only in the righteousness of Christ that we receive grace to speak pure words.

SILVER TRIED IN THE FURNACE OF EARTH, PURIFIED SEVEN TIMES

Silver is often used in the Bible as a symbol of purging and refinement (Proverbs 25:11, Proverbs 2:3-4). In order for us to rightly testify of Jesus and release encounter through prophecy, we must grant allowance for the nature of the Word that is Christ (John 1:1) to reform every other contrary nature in our lives. This process sets the right environment in the vessel. The flow of God's imrah through us cannot be rightly fulfilled if it was never fully incubated in us. It is of interest that God will take great lengths to ensure that His prophetic people develop yielded hearts (e.g Jonah), as the imrah of Yahweh must first go in before it can go through (Luke 6:45). Oftentimes, this is the reason why many see little impact in their prophetic ministry. The cares of life dam up the well, frustrating the full work of the Word to produce transformation. I call this building with wood, hay and straw, and I borrow it from Paul's analogy as he spoke to the Corinthians (1 Corinthians 3:9-15). He wanted to challenge them about how they went about their work with the Lord, not being carnal but walking in the superior quality of life that is afforded in Christ. Here he highlights materials that refract and reflect light when speaking of the superior life (gold, silver, precious stones), and this is critical when we consider our calling as God's oracles, shining His light (John 8:12). Choosing otherwise means that the abundant measure of the prophetic gusher is not realized as it is challenged by wood (a biblical symbol that speaks to our self-will), hay (a biblical symbol that speaks to a life of flippancy), straw (a biblical symbol that speaks to fleshly living), and instead of the hearer receiving the wellspring of life they are left with something less. This cannot be so for us if we truly want to be right representatives of Jesus' heart. We must be mindful that sin and self (products of the world nature) will always create barrenness and death (Romans 6:23), but sanctity and selflessness (products of the Word nature) yield great reward for the prophesier and receiver alike (Matthew 5:8).

Weighing your prophetic release

In Psalm 29, the Psalmist continues to give us insight about the voice of the Lord. He describes the voice of the Lord as nothing short of amazing, and uses words such as powerful and full of majesty to capture the grandeur of God speaking (Psalm 29:4). If you followed through with your assignment from our last chapter, you will discover many attributes of God's voice mentioned here. Not only that, but you will appreciate the standard to which God measures His Voice, and it is this standard that we must continue to weigh our prophetic release by. This becomes our mirror of evaluation and scale for discernment, and as we study the scripture below we will come to appreciate the revelation of the psalmist and what it communicates to us.

> "The voice of the Lord is powerful; The voice of the Lord is full of majesty."
> Psalm 29:4 (NKJV)

Let's look at some definitions below:

- The word for *powerful* used here in its original language is **kowach (ko'-akh)**. It means to batter down, to construct, to multiply, potency to produce, wealthy, creative power, able to deliver, limitless resources.
- The word for *full of majesty* used here in its original language is **hadar (haw-dawr')**. It means magnificent, glorious, honorable, noble, the fear/terror of the Lord, royalty and holy.

When we release the voice of the Lord via prophesying, we must measure our prophetic words from this perspective. Are they full of majesty, bearing witness to the magnificence of God? Are they powerful, battering down strongholds and creating hope and destiny for others? Do those who receive cry out 'Glory' at the end of your prophetic release (Psalm 29:9)? Are they overwhelmed by the revealing of their hearts, and give praise to God in your midst (1 Corinthians 14:24-25)? This is what we must press in for as we grow in the prophetic. Our delivery of God's word must be weighty with such things, giving testimony to the truth of His word. When we hold His word with high esteem in our hearts, and our faith for encounter for the person receiving is greater than our fear of embarrassing ourselves, then amazing results are the fruit born from our witness.

Sharpening your delivery

One thing I have come to recognize in prophetic ministry, is the fact that God chooses to use us at our various levels of proficiencies and gifting (Romans 12:6), and this includes our ability to communicate. Some people are better communicators than others, but let me say to you that communication is not just a gift but rather a skill that you can develop and work on. We have spoken extensively about God working in us as we lean on Him, but He is practical and provides tools that we can utilize to work on ourselves to become more efficient in our service. Consider the story of the talents if at any point you forget that God is not the only one in the story called to labor, but He has called you as a co-laborer who will multiply with wisdom what He puts in your hand (Matthew 25:14-30). So let's look at some practical measures below.

WHAT IS YOUR BODY SAYING THAT YOUR MOUTH IS NOT?

First and utmost in communication, one must understand that eighty-five percent (85%) of your ability to communicate effectively is based upon more than just words, but other dynamics that I have listed below:

- Facial expressions
- Hand movement
- Body movements
- Vocal inflection and quality
- Eyes and what they communicate
- Words and how they are used
- Attitude that reflects the character of Jesus

Your body often tells more than your mouth, therefore if you are going to communicate on His behalf with impact, consider these dynamics presented here. What is your face saying to the person as you are speaking? If God instructs you to communicate His heart of kindness and love, you should rather refrain from frowning while speaking. You should also ensure that your fingers are not pointing as this is seen as a judgmental/accusatory posture, but rather open your palm and gesture it towards them. This ensures a more relaxed posture for the person on the receiving end, as receiving a prophetic word can already be unnerving. Resting your hand on their shoulder gently, and utilizing vocal inflection (a suitable tone) that matches the context of what you are communicating is also important. Again, imagine God desiring to speak through you to reassure His child of His heart of love towards them, but you end up speaking with fiery fervency like a captain to his unit that are ready to jump into the battlefield. This obviously does not fit the context, so be mindful of your tone and cadence. You don't want that person to shut down and have in their mind how they're going to escape you, because of poor presentation and vocal misalignment. Dress and show up with great body language that matches the content and heart of what God is speaking.

INTERCEDING INTO THE FIVE SPHERES OF HUMAN LIFE

Intercession is critical if you are going to release impact that shifts lives. If we remember Marie from our first chapter and how God was able to make significant impact on Francia through her, you will remember the shift occurred because of intercession. When we show care for others by taking on the character of Christ as their intercessor (Hebrews 7:25), then we will see great results! Our key scripture reminds us that the testimony of Jesus is the spirit of prophecy, and if we are to release the spirit of prophecy, then like Jesus, we are going to have to make intercession for others our priority. These five spheres can be used to ask God questions concerning any person,

Intercession is critical if you are going to release impact.

known or unknown. Usually as my day commences, I pray to God to speak to me about people who may contact me during the day, or those who I may come across as I go from one place to another. I intentionally ask Him to reveal to me His wisdom and His desire for them. I make this part of my daily intercession, believing for opportunity that will lead to encounter. Remember, you want to ask not because your desire is to be seen as accurate and to be known as someone who hears the Lord, but you are doing so because of your passion for Jesus to be glorified in their life. As you ask as Jesus said to do (Matthew 7:7, Mark 11:24), just be sensitive to His leading. Sometimes for me it may seem like I have not received anything in my time of morning prayer, however when I am in the moment of engagement with others, Holy Spirit quickly informs my heart right there on the spot with expediency. In yielding to Him as His vessel, I have set the atmosphere of my day by inviting Him in to bring genuine change to the lives of others. You can do the same too! Let us look as these five spheres below:

- The person's relationship with God (releasing affirmation or a challenge to go deeper)
- The person's health (either their soul or physical body)
- The person's calling in life (area of ministry and anointing)
- The person's family and friends (plus their relation to them)
- The person's financial situation (what is God saying and intending for them)

Ask and it will be given to you

As you look over these areas, be sure to ask God questions. In respect to the first sphere which is relationship, ask the Lord if He desires to release affirmation to them and encourage them in respect to how far they have come? Does He desire to take them deeper, and if so, what does that look like? In regards to their health, ask Him to open your eyes to any person suffering with infirmity that may come your way. Ask God to reveal these sickly conditions to your heart so you can pray about it. Matters of health are just as much a matter of damaged emotions and a broken heart as they are a bodily infirmity, and this is an area that many deal with to some degree. Let not only the gift of revelation inform you of such circumstances, but also allow the gift of wisdom to guide you in revealing Jesus' heart to that person in such sensitive situations (Ephesians 1:17). Even if what you may see may be dark and hurtful, speak life and encouragement as the Word commands (1 Corinthians 14:3). Retelling the dark and hurtful scenario can cause more damage, and unseasoned prophesiers usually fall prey to this. Remember that you are there to release solutions to problems, and not reinforce them. Also ask Him to reveal their concerns in regards to their financial situation and felt needs, and what He would say to them personally concerning that. Remember, demonic thieves like to hide in the dark as their purpose is to steal, kill and destroy. However, you have come to bring the abundant life of Christ to those folks' situations (John 10:10). Ask God to bring into the light anything functioning in the dark, for He is faithful to heal what is revealed, breaking the demonic assignment!

Another area is that person's calling in life, or for a certain specific season of their life. What does God want to speak into regarding that. Many often feel hopeless and lost in this area, and I have found that this is one of the key areas that God speaks most to me about when it comes to others. That's probably because it was a driving factor in my own salvation and search for Christ. I love when I can engage them and share what I sense the Lord revealing, then to hear that person say that it is the exact thing they have been thinking about or believing to walk in. This grants confidence and gives them a booster shot of faith to step out and trust the Lord in their unique calling, and this confirming power of prophecy is so needed today. We need more laborers out in the harvest field doing what they have been assigned by God to do!

There is also the area of family and friends. Many people are carrying the burden of others or personal pain from family situations or broken friendships. Ask the Lord for specifics concerning this as you prepare your heart to be used by Him. Many people that interact with me often do not present their own needs, but those of their families. Having a word that is in season for them and that can help them strategically navigate those troubled waters can be extremely helpful in impacting not just the individual, but other family members and friends for Jesus. Remember, a word fitly spoken is like apples of gold in settings of silver (Proverbs 25:11).

Out of the boat – dates, times and specifics

As you step out and allow the Lord occasion to use you, your prophetic service to others will grow. You will be overwhelmed at how good God can be to others through you, and extremely fulfilled to see them draw closer to Jesus. This will encourage your faith to become even sharper in your witness and desire to release the spirit of prophecy. As you do so, there may be times where you don't get it right. If getting it right was always the case, Paul would not have instructed the church at Corinth to have some prophesy and others judge or carefully examine what was being said (1 Corinthians 14:29).

Indeed, to launch out in faith we must step out of the boat of our comfort zone like Peter, but do not give up on your journey in the supernatural dimensions of Christ just because you sank at one time. Peter surely did not! Keep putting to use the spiritual gifts God has given you as you abide in Him, and they will grow sharper and clearer (Hebrews 5:14). Stay accountable to spiritual authority, and keep challenging and pushing yourself into deeper levels of faith. It is those who stop because of one moment of stumbling, that end up living a mediocre and dull spiritual life (Ecclesiastes 10:10). Here are a few nuggets to consider as we close this chapter.

We must step out of the boat of our comfort.

Revelation is No Respecter of Persons

There is no age or limit on revelation. Believe for full revelation no matter what level you minister at prophetically. At the same time, remain humble to learn from your successes as well as mistakes.

Maturity and Responsibility

Before driving a car, you have to be a certain age and possess certain skills to obtain your license. A similar principle is true in certain areas of ministry. Public ministry of dates, times and specifics is reserved for skilled mature ministry which has been seasoned over time. However, keep learning and growing, not being afraid to step out in faith along the way.

Accuracy

When you make a mistake in your prophetic accuracy, that is all you have done. You are not a false prophet. False prophesy is being wrong in spirit and content. Remain humble and learn from your mistakes. My policy at Bible School was this, "Lord, thank you when I am accurate but thank you even so when I miss it since it is another opportunity to work humility in me."

Details Increase Faith for Both You and the Hearer

The more details that you give, the clearer the word is. Also, giving relevant details will increase the faith of those receiving the ministry as well as your own. Go for it! Words of knowledge can really help in this area of ministry and will establish a powerful witness.

I remember back in 2003 when I accompanied Apostle Gale Sheehan of Christian International on a ministry trip in Alabama. He would usually take a few students from our Bible School along with him on these weekend trips, and I was one of seven students on that particular trip. We drove from Santa Rosa Beach Florida to the church in Montgomery, Alabama, and we arrived there the Friday ready to minister. Some of us who were staying by the Pastor's home (that included me), went there first to put down our stuff before heading over to the church. As students we couldn't all stay at fancy hotels, but these trips offered ministry experience and a change of scenery so we usually grabbed the opportunity when it afforded itself. On the first night, I remember Apostle Gale had us all stand before the church and do prophetic call-out ministry. This is when prophetic ministers would take the time to call out individuals one by one and minister to them individually. It would usually transpire for about 30-40 minutes, with each person having three or four chances to minister. On my last go, I remember stepping out by faith and asking if someone by the name of Marcia was present, and I went on to encourage her to come down to the altar. After repeating myself about three times, no one stepped forward, and I felt for a second that maybe I didn't hear God on that one. Embarrassment and discouragement tried to paralyze me, but I quickly moved on to call someone else out and prophesied to them. However, I couldn't shake the feeling that God had impressed on me that a lady by that name was there.

The next day, as we rose for breakfast at the Pastor's house, he came over to the table with excitement in his step. We could all tell something was up. He held to the chair and leaned over at us saying, "You know that lady Marcia who you called by name last night, well I just got a call from the church administrator stating that a lady by the name of Marcia called to say she was on her way to service last night but had car troubles. She had to stay over at a motel, but wanted to reach out concerning service times today, because she intends to still make it. Upon hearing this my heart leaped and my face lit up! I hadn't missed it, praise God! We had a good laugh thinking about the faithfulness of God as a student body, and later that night I had the opportunity to minister to Marcia. In fact, half way down the church aisle as I ministered several words of knowledge to her, she fell under the power of the Spirit of God. God gave her exact details about a contract and papers she was awaiting that had to do with urgent family inheritance matters, and a long drawn out circumstance with her lawyer. She testified afterward that every word was correct, and now she had strategy from heaven to go back to the matter with. Isn't God amazing!? This definitely increased her faith, but the way that everything unfolded increased mine as well. This is why when we can't seem to trace God, we can always trust Him. He is faithful! Don't be afraid to step out and trust Him.

Using Dates, Times and Specifics

Be wary of trying to impress others as opposed to obeying God. Be wary also of fear that will try to antagonize your spirit from sharing the full counsel of God. Say what you believe He is speaking, nothing more and nothing less. If He is challenging you to step out with dates and times, then trust His leadership. Remember, always be more expectant of God revealing the glory of His Son to that individual than entertaining the fear of missing the mark.

For The Profit of All

The manifestation of the Holy Spirit through you is for the profit of all (1 Corinthians 12:7). Keep your focus on honoring God and blessing His people, being wary of giving attention on your performance. When you make it about you, your impact will fall through.

Spread Promises and Not Pollution

Prophecy is for exhortation, edification and comfort (1 Corinthians 14:3). Even when the dynamic is corrective, it must still be redemptive. We must therefore have the right attitude. Having the right word but the wrong attitude ultimately leads to disaster, and will result in the impact of the word diminishing. Despite the circumstances that are happening around you, always welcome the Lord to purify what is stirring within you.

Surround Yourself With The Right Environment

Bad company still corrupts good character, and faithless company can be a wet blanket over the fire of your heart. Surround yourself with people of faith that are moving in the dimensions of God that you are believing for in your own life. I have found that the prophetic and other gifts of the Spirit are more often caught than taught, and surrounding yourself with other hungry hearts for the things of God will ensure your fire is stirred and faith encouraged. Even Jesus was concerned about the environment. He was not a controller of people, but He did control the surroundings, often asking those without faith to leave the room (Matthew 9:25).

What do we say to these things?

Our journey through this chapter would have helped you see how a life lived in His Presence works out itself in a practical way to touch His people. We have to be congruent with Heaven but connected in our witness to others, so utilize the methods given with proper motive and prepare for massive transformation. I'm so excited for you! Let's not be lights hidden under a bushel, but let us all shine for Jesus (Matthew 5:14-16). May the Lamb that was slain receive the reward of His suffering!

Go Deeper

In life we wrestle with pride when it comes to letting our needs be known. We are not good at asking. However Jesus stresses this mode of dependence if we are to receive from God. He also practiced it, as he prayed to the Father on many occasions and publicly asked the Father to grant certain requests in confirming who He was. Do you also struggle with asking, and how do you plan to become a more consistent asker, seeker and knocker?

Which of the five spheres resonates with how God has most used you to speak into the lives of others?

CHAPTER FIVE

Marked For The Marketplace

Made For Great Adventures With God

"We are ambassadors for Christ, as though
God were pleading through us: we implore you
on Christ's behalf, be reconciled to God."
2 Corinthians 5:20 (NKJV)

Am I agitated or accustomed?

The Apostle Paul experienced dynamic adventures with God throughout the book of Acts, and one that is of particular interest to our subject is his arrival to Athens (Acts 17:16). Prefacing his arrival there, Paul had just been forced to flee Thessalonica and Berea due to a sect of Jews who turned the townspeople against him through lies and falsehoods, as they were envious of his impact for Jesus (Acts 17:5-15). These dangerous threats were indeed weapons that were formed against him, however they did not prosper. They only caused Paul to spread the message of Jesus' triumph to other territories. Consider this result when you are in seasons where you feel most under fire from hell. Know that God is in the background executing His purpose! Paul later found this out, as his arrival in Athens opened up an effectual door for the gospel while gifting to Paul life long friendships that would aid him in his work for years to come.

So what is so special about this arrival in Athens? Well upon reading the text in Acts 17, you will discover an interesting word that stands out in verse 16 of this chapter. It says that while he waited for the arrival of his co-laborers, Silas and Timothy, his spirit was provoked within him because he saw that the city was given over to idols. This provocation caused Paul to enter into the marketplace on a daily basis to reason with those there (Acts 17:17). As the story continues, we see that his engagement in the marketplace caught the attention of some who invited him into other influential forums so that they could indulge in his message with greater attention and numbers present (Acts 17:19). What an amazing open door to walk in his ambassadorship in Christ!

Many believers today have grown so accustomed to the culture around them that their spirit has become dull and desensitized to the reality of opportunity that awaits them everyday. The truth is, 99% of us function in the marketplace, and here resides our opportunity to be lights to a world steeped in darkness. You can't just say, "Well I'll wait on my pastor to reach them." The truth is, the very word pastor literally means a shepherd, and I have never seen a shepherd produce sheep. In the wise words of Dr. Bill Hamon, sheep produce sheep! We have to go out there as His sheep who hear His voice (John 10:27) and reveal Him to a dying world.

I have never seen a shepherd produce sheep.

Now there are three key principles in Paul's efforts here in Athens that you cannot afford to miss. These will help energize you in boldly engaging the culture around you.

1 **Don't Overanalyze Opportunity**—Paul did not need a now word from the Lord to get engaged in revealing truth to those in the marketplace. He only needed to be provoked by the tragedy of uninformed souls around him and the deceitful schemes of Satan that he saw in operation. As a man who had just survived chastisement, death threats and being chased out of two other territories, you might imagine that he would think twice about moving on this provocation in his spirit. Maybe even to reconsider engaging, and probably waiting on his friends to arrive before getting into action. However, what we witness is a man who did not overthink the opportunity that was before him. He trusted that the groan in his heart was God pleading through him to a lost world, imploring them to be reconciled to God as our key scripture of this chapter implies. What can we learn from this?

Well, sometimes we overanalyze our opportunity to make impact and then we end up paralyzed. Don't overanalyze your opportunity to make a difference, but trust the groan of God in your spirit. It is often said that analysis overdone results in paralysis, and many have been crippled from making a difference due to this misdemeanor of interrupting spiritual fervency with soulish hesitancy, then labeling it as wisdom. How strange would that theological stance be to the ears of the Apostle Paul! Friends, if we say we are abiding in God's affection then we must be arrested by what holds His attention. This world that He so loved, that He sent His only begotten Son to (John 3:16), is still before His ever roaming eyes as He searches for hearts in every place (Proverbs 15:3, 2 Chronicles 16:9). May you be freed of unhealthy deliberation and move upon that inner provocation.

2 **Be Consistent and Committed**—Paul made this engagement a daily practice (Acts 17:17). There is something to be said about staying committed even when the initial result is not what you expect. Though he was called a babbler and was scoffed at by some in the marketplace during

his attempts to reason with them, Paul stayed connected to his assignment. Like any of us, he could have felt disengaged by not getting the type of result that he experienced as with previous occasions, like back in Berea where his word was received with all readiness (Acts 17:11). He could have become dissuaded and think in his mind that maybe he missed what God really called him to do here at Athens. However, he stayed consistent and engaged, coming out day after day to attend to his call to be a light in the midst of darkness. His consistency eventually opened a greater door before a greater audience, and it was there that some believed and had an encounter with God (Acts 17:34).

The lesson here is consistency. Not every heart will change with one moment of ministry. Let the Lord work patience in your heart concerning His processes in the lives of others, and stay faithful to the task. I have seen this truth so often in my life when stepping out to aid others. In one of my many stories, my heart was fired up as I went to work as a young adult during a summer internship, and I had determined that I would make a step to minister to my boss. As mentioned in the last chapter, I prayed God would open up an opportunity during the day to engage him, and He did just that. In the middle of the day, my boss called a fellow colleague and myself into his office to discuss some work related deadlines. After the conversation ended and we were being dismissed, I asked him if he had five minutes of his time to afford for a quick chat. He said yes, and allowed me to stay in the room while my other colleague exited. This was the opportunity I had been believing for! I shared with him that I was praying for him, and that I wanted to encourage him with a special message that would only take a few minutes. He agreed, and there I shared about what God told me concerning his family. In my heart, my hope was that it would pierce him so deeply that he would give his heart to Jesus on the spot, but that didn't happen. I was really hoping for something dramatic, but he just sat and received the word with a semi-stoic look on his face. The only peace of mind I received before I got up to leave was him saying that what I shared was very interesting. I left thinking to myself, *What in the world could that mean? Should I have really said what I said?* However, though it left me pondering for a few days, I made up in my mind to keep praying for him.

About a week later he called me into his office, and asked the rest of the staff not to be disturbed. He then began to share about what was said and how it would not leave his mind. He was very curious to know how I could have known certain matters about his children, and how the word was right on target for them. Upon further conversation, I discovered that certain matters that I shared with him had not transpired at the time of my sharing, but did in the days thereafter. God was being proactive in preparing him to know some matters that would soon come to pass, and when it did happen it deeply convicted him. This then opened up further opportunity for me to pray for him and be his counsel until my time at the summer job was over. He showed me special favor to the point that other staff members began to interrogate me about his reasons for having me in his office so often. They had never seen it done before. Their inquisitiveness then opened opportunity for me to be a light to them individually, and soon after they were asking me to prepare devotional studies for them in the morning before work commenced. What an incredible ripple effect!

> ## Don't let an unmet expectation stifle your determination and suspend your contribution!

This story always encourages me to not judge things according to my natural mind, but trust God's ways. He doesn't always reveal to us His complete plan, but He calls us to have faith in Him as we are being used for His glory. It is a constant reminder that we all may sow and water, but at the end of the day it is the Lord who brings the increase and makes things grow (1 Corinthians 3:7). Don't stop being a light friends! God's seed of purpose in the heart of another just needs a bit more water until it springs forth. Stay faithful and don't let an unmet expectation stifle your determination and suspend your contribution.

3 **Connect with Palatable Clarity**—When Paul's daily visits to the marketplace opened up opportunity for him to stand before a wider audience, he used the language and the imagery of their culture to communicate his conviction. We observe that the altar to their unknown God becomes his springboard to introduce them to the one true God (Acts 17:22-24). The language of their poets also becomes the wind in the sail of his exegesis regarding the true God's nature (Acts 17:28). This was tactful, as he disclosed deep revelation in a way that was tangible and palatable to his hearers (Acts 17:22-34). In similar fashion, when we are releasing prophetic life to others we should embrace similar awareness so that God's utterance is not bloated in language or acts they do not understand. Our sound must be clear (1 Corinthians 14:8), and we must never assume that our environment and level of exposure to Christian dialogue is the same for others.

> **Our sound must be clear, and we must never assume that our environment and level of exposure to Christian dialogue is the same for others.**

Many are unchurched, and may be not give you an ear if you appear to be a spooky spiritual, holier than thou charismatic. Leave your prophetic accent at home, and hold off from the thundering statement of "Thus saith the Lord." You can share simply by means of regular conversation and ask God for creativity in communicating His heart in way that is palatable and clear to the hearer. Let God use the natural things in the environment to help inform your spirit as well. You may be surprised at how it launches you deeper into further insight.

In my story in the previous point with my boss, one of the things I noticed when I came into his office was his family pictures. It immediately impressed upon my heart how important his family was to him, and God used my observation to give me further information right there in his office. This confirmed what I had already sensed, but allowed me to believe for more details as my heart felt invigorated by the confirmation. It also allowed me to know where God wanted to take up emphasis as pertains to the five spheres of the human life. I had other things to share outside of family, but that was peripheral to the main issue God wanted to target. In the end, what I gave to him in the room far surpassed what I had already received in my time of prayer at home. I encourage you to be open to the springboards God may bring your way as you speak into the lives of others. In my prophetic engagement with others, many words have started with movie references or current trends that God would have me to use as a point of reference while giving further insight. This often connects with their heart, as God knows what appeals to them.

"But if all prophesy, and an unbeliever or an uninformed person comes in,
he is convinced by all, he is convicted by all."
1 Corinthians 14:24

BUILDING WHILE YOU ARE BUILDING

Many are afraid to use their spiritual gifting outside the four walls of the church. This fear is not just due to the fact that you are amongst those who are different and don't believe like you, but it is also demonically inspired. The enemy knows the harvest is ripe and will try to intimidate you with thoughts of apprehension and preconceived rejection to make you compromise valuable opportunities. Satan always trades in such fear and lies, and his desire is to keep you at bay with the great power you possess in Christ. However, Jesus' reminder to us is that the harvest is indeed ripe, which means that it is not difficult to reap. Paul realized this when he moved on from Athens to Corinth. There he was building tents and at the same time building the Kingdom. He had a natural job, but he understood his spiritual assignment. In this record, we see that though he tried his best to impact the religious, he realized that greater fruitfulness came when he went to the unchurched. As you read the scripture below, may you hear the voice of Jesus speaking to you as He spoke to Paul. May you hear Him say, **"Do not be afraid and do not keep silent!"** May you be supernaturally empowered to make your mark in the marketplace.

"After these things Paul departed from Athens and went to Corinth. And he found a certain Jew named Aquila, born in Pontus, who had recently come from Italy with his wife Priscilla (because Claudius had commanded all the Jews to depart from Rome); and he came to them. So, because he was of the same trade, he stayed with them and worked; for by occupation they were tentmakers. And he reasoned in the synagogue every Sabbath, and persuaded both Jews and Greeks. When Silas and Timothy had come from Macedonia, Paul was compelled by the Spirit, and testified to the Jews that Jesus is the Christ. But when they opposed him and blasphemed, he shook his garments and said to them, 'Your blood be upon your own heads; I am clean. From now on I will go to the Gentiles.' And he departed from there and entered the house of a certain man named Justus, one who worshiped God, whose house was next door to the synagogue. Then Crispus, the ruler of the synagogue, believed on the Lord with all his household. And many of the Corinthians, hearing, believed and were baptized. Now the Lord spoke to Paul in the night by a vision, 'Do not be afraid, but speak, and do not keep silent; for I am with you, and no one will attack you to hurt you; for I have many people in this city.' And he continued there a year and six months, teaching the word of God among them."

Acts 18:1-11

Go Deeper

Have you ever struggled with the paralysis of analysis? Has it ever caused you to miss a valuable opportunity? If so, what steps are you committed to taking to ensure that you are not robbed of opportunities going forward? How will you determine to overcome fear with Godly courage?

Write two ways that you expect God to use you this week to prophetically impact the life of an unchurched friend or family member. When you are finished take 30 minutes to pray for these opportunities. Ask the Lord to give you details of what you should say even before you meet these individuals. Ask Him to speak to you in dreams and visions about the opportunities and individuals (Psalm 19:2).

CHAPTER SIX

It Shall Surely Come To Pass

From Articulation To Actualization

"For I am the LORD. I speak, and the word that
I shall speak shall come to pass."
Ezekiel 12:25 (NKJV)

The nature of prophecy

From Genesis to Revelation, the Word of God is full of prophetic promises that are either conditional or unconditional in nature. When the term *unconditional prophecies* is used, it infers that which has been determined by God to come to pass, despite human intervention. God will perform it and no one can stop it! As seen in the prophetic unveiling of Nebuchadnezzar's dream (Daniel 2:31-45), many of these unconditional words were spoken concerning the unfolding of world events, God's sovereign plan for the nations of the earth, and of matters concerning the summation of the end of the age. *Conditional prophecies*, however, are quite different, and the term implies that there is a human component of participation that is necessary to see the prophetic word come to pass. It carries with it a sense of being contingent on human response, action or inaction, and this is what we will explore as we address personal prophecies that have been spoken over your life. These fall under this category of *conditional* that indulges your participation, and your obedience to God is critical in moving the prophecy from the realm of articulation to actualization. Now this is by no means an act of coercing your prophetic words to come to pass—God has already determined four dynamics related to the purpose of the personal prophetic word and how it manifests. Understanding these dynamics will help you discern your responsibility in coming into alignment with your assignment.

The dynamics of unveiling personal prophecy

1 **God's personal prophetic word is designed to first prepare you, before it presents you.** His priority is the process of inwardly refining you, before releasing outward manifestation in your life. In Psalm 105:19, it says that before the word of the Lord came to pass concerning Joseph, it tried him. The statement *tried him* that is used here in the Hebrew means *to refine* or *to make pure*. We know Joseph had mighty prophetic dreams that unveiled great purpose and destiny regarding his future (Genesis 37:5-11), but the unfolding of the word happened in such a way that was quite unimaginable to the dreamer. He had to undergo refinement of character on the inside before he could manage the crown of destiny on the outside. Despite the rigors of the process over a lengthy period of time, Joseph didn't grow bitter but he allowed the process to make him better (Genesis 50:20), and God was able to present him into the full authority of the prophetic decree over his life with him walking in right perspective. This is critical as we contend for God's promises in our

life. We must ensure that we are allowing the process internally, as it will determine what is then manifested externally. If we kick against the goads and resist His process we can delay matters of destiny for ourselves (Acts 26:14), or like King Saul, even forfeit them (1 Samuel 15:26). I have known folk that received powerful prophetic words but did not wait on God's processing, and rather strived in their own strength to see those words manifest. Many received what they thought was the fruition of the word coming to pass, but realized in time that it was more of a heavy burden than a heavenly gift. As with Abram and Sarah, this striving to manifest the word in our own way only leads to us birthing an Ishmael instead of an Isaac, and Ishmaels produce heartache and make the manifestation of the promise even more stressful (Genesis 16:1-13). Obedience to God is indeed better than our own idea of sacrifice (1 Samuel 15:22), and our willingness to obey Him in the hidden place will grant us the strength that we need when He escalates the promise in the public eye. Remember that God's ultimate purpose is to conform you to the image of His Son (Romans 8:29), so do what is necessary to ensure you are yielding to His inner processes. By doing so, you can come into alignment with God's timetable for the outward manifestation of the word over your life, and even hasten it (2 Peter 3:11-12).

2 **God's personal prophetic word to you has a systematic process of escalation.** The prophet Zechariah reminds us not to despise the day of small things (Zechariah 4:10), and personal prophecy will often lead us into a journey that starts with incremental steps. It is true that our first faith step can feel like a gigantic leap of faith, but we soon realize that the journey does not start with the full manifestation of the promise. It is unveiled in a series of episodes that coordinate with our obedience. Like Abram receiving his personal prophecy to leave the land of his fathers so that he might become a great nation (Genesis 12:1-3), we know that the full manifestation of this promise took decades. This timeframe was

constructed by incremental steps of faith, and God meeting with Him at junctures in the journey to test him and confirm his obedience (Genesis 22:1-18). These meetings or encounters were for the purpose of renewing his vigor, granting increase in the knowledge of God, and revealing to him the next steps as he was faithful in completing previous directives. Such a calculated process is also seen in the life of Saul of Tarsus, who after his encounter with Jesus more often used his Roman name, Paul. Upon this encounter with the resurrected Lord on the road to Damascus as told in Acts 9, he was later prophesied over by a disciple of Jesus called Ananias in a nearby city. The Lord had given Ananias a word for Paul, and it revealed Paul's purpose and mission to bear the name of Christ before Gentiles, kings and the children of Israel (Acts 9:15). However, the fulfillment of this word did not happen immediately. Paul took several years to prepare (Galatians 1:11-20) before he was commissioned to commence the first mission connected to this revelation (Acts 13:1-12). The part of the prophetic word that foretold his ministry before kings transpired in ways Paul probably did not expect, with him being imprisoned and thus gaining an audience with this particular group Jesus highlighted (Acts 24-26). It goes to show that not only is the revealing of destiny a step by step process of obedience, but it can also be unpredictable with regard to what we hear and how it manifests. God's ways are surely higher than ours (Isaiah 55:8-9). Jesus also clues us in to this reality of how God unlocks prophetic destiny by stating that whoever can be trusted with very little can also be trusted with much (Luke 16:10-12). Speaking concerning earthly wealth and spiritual commodity, He implies that one's management of the mediocre determines how one will further manage the majestic. The trend we see here is that despite the circumstances, faithfulness is the key that unlocks doors to more prominent responsibility in destiny fulfillment. Stay faithful where you are planted until God opens the door. Beware of the fact that the devil can also present "opportunity" (Matthew 4:8-10), and this kind will provoke you to mess up God's best by moving outside the certainty of God's peace. Allow the fruit of the Spirit cultivated in you (Galatians 5:22-23) to confirm the move of the Spirit through you (1 Corinthians 2:10).

> **Whoever can be trusted with very little can also be trusted with much.**

3 **God's personal prophetic word is designed as a weapon that can be used to wage effective warfare.** As a seasoned counselor, I have come across many who battle frustration regarding destiny and not seeing the manifestation of their prophetic promises. This is often due to them having disregarded them by shelving them away. They receive a prophetic word or promise from the Lord and they do not take the time to deeply consider it and use it as part of their prayer life. We must be careful not to quench the Spirit in our lives by despising prophecies (1 Thessalonians 5:19-21). My family and I have had several prophetic promises we've had to war with to see God's breakthrough in the natural realm. When we say that we war with them, what we mean is that we get the prophetic words out and listen to them together. Then we write them out, and use them as part of our prayer time. The reason we do this is so that we can gather the full context of what God has said. When you write, you give opportunity for your eyes to engage the material and not just your ears via listening. Hearing and listening via our auditory function furnishes us with the highlights of what was said, but reading engages the eyes and helps us capture the context of what was said with greater clarity. Again, hearing leaves us with the highlights/key points but reading leaves us with the context! Whenever I'm asked for counsel about a prophetic word that

someone has trouble understanding, I implore the individual to go away and write it out. In almost every circumstance, the seeker returns with the understanding, and has the clarity needed to war effectively. Remember, the Word (*Rhema*) of God is the sword of the spirit (Ephesians 6:17), and you have to know how to use your sword effectively in the battle. Even our children get engaged in this activity with us, and we have seen doors of destiny swing wide open as we come together to agree and wage a good warfare with what God has spoken and promised. In the triumph of Christ the devil has indeed lost the war (Colossians 2:15), but that doesn't mean that he will automatically surrender his territory in the battle. You must exert force in your prayer life in standing on what God has said (Matthew 11:12), using your authority to trample serpents and scorpions that are demonic entities of resistance in the unseen realm (Luke 10:19, Ephesians 6:12). King David was a great example of this. In 2 Samuel 7, history recalls David coming to a place where he had rest from his enemies, but his heart was burning him in respect to further purpose. He was agitated by the location of the ark of God which was in a tent, compared to his personal living arrangements in a home of cedar. I really love this about David! He was not just enamored with his own blessings and personal affairs, but was truly a man after God's own heart. May God cause our hearts to burn just the same, provoking us beyond the periphery of our own affairs! The story goes on with Nathan the prophet entering the conversation. He had overheard the desire of David's heart, and God came and spoke to him regarding a personal prophecy that was to be spoken to the King (2 Samuel 7:4-17). Upon hearing this word, David engages the prophetic word in prayer, and proactively wages a good warfare by making specific declarations that align with the prophecy.

Having received revelation that God would have it to be his offspring who would build a house for His Name, David was delivered from striving in his flesh according to the desire of his heart through offering unnecessary sacrifices that didn't align with God's purpose. Instead, he was able to make preparation to aid Solomon with the means to go about doing what he desired to do for the Lord. What an amazing example of how engaging the prophetic to wage a good warfare can deliver us from good intentions that are not God's direction.

4 **God always encourages the process of confirmation in authenticating the validity of personal prophecy.** As you step out to obey what you believe God has said, it is important to verify that He is the source of the inspiration you received. In 2 Corinthians 13:1, Paul gives us doctrinal guidance in understanding that every word shall be established by the mouth of two or three witnesses, and it grants a framework for authenticating the validity of personal prophecy. When Paul says "every word" the greek translation for *word* is **rhema.** A *rhema word* is a message inspired by God that is personal to you and specific to your current situation, while offering no contradiction with the written word of God (i.e *Logos*). The nature of personal prophecy is very much that of a rhema word, and in order for it to be established it must be confirmed by the mouth of two or three witnesses. By its nature, prophecy is both forthtelling (interpreting the purposes of God and divinely revealing insight of God's word beyond surface information) and foretelling (speaking into future events). Concerning the latter, it can also speak to plans the Holy Spirit may have already revealed to you personally about your future (John 16:13). God may also cause other prophetic individuals to speak the same things over your life, or cause you to have multiple personal confirmations so to strengthen your faith, like Gideon in walking out His purpose (Judges 6:36-40). Always have at least one confirmation so that the word can be established. It is a principle that is respected in both the seen and unseen realms, and having it present will grant you security and safety as you walk out the call of God on your life. You should also bring the prophetic word before mature prophetic counsel so that they can help you weigh it before making sudden moves. Sudden moves can

be geographical movements, changing careers, risky business deals, etc. Note that God will never tell you to do something that is in disagreement with the tenets of the written Word. Such a word is not prophetic but very pathetic! With respect to sharing your word with a spiritual authority that flows in prophecy, I can't recommend this step enough. It is a biblical safety-net, and was practiced in the early church as seen with the Apostle Paul when he received certain revelations from Holy Spirit. He said that he wanted to ensure he presented it to the senior leaders at Jerusalem (Peter and James, brother of Jesus, Galatians 1:18-19), so to be sure that he was not running his race in vain (Galatians 2:2). If the great Apostle Paul had to verify his own prophetic insight, then I think we all can take a leaf from his book and ensure that we do not step out on something that God has not called us to do. As King Solomon states, in the multitude of counsel there is safety (Proverbs 11:14).

Actualization is an ongoing process

God is very aware of what is best for His people, and I am thankful that He does not microwave His work. In an age where we are so accustomed to instant deliveries of our purchases and air fryer dishes, God reminds us that His ways are not our ways, but far more significant and beneficial for the greatest prosperity of all parties involved (Isaiah 55:8-9). In saying this, I want to remind you that the journey to actualization is more about what is being formed in you, than what is materializing around you (Romans 8:30). The formation of Christlike character and godliness is of greater gain to our eternal posture than any other, and you must take off the world's lens of success and let God anoint your eyes so you can see (Revelation 3:18).

Go Deeper

It's time to go back to Chapter Two and reexamine the principles of authentic demonstration. After a quick read through refresher go ahead and rate yourself once again. Place your new rating below. On a scale of 1-10 (with 1 being pretty poor and 10 being superb), how would you rate the quality of your motive, your mindset and your ministry?

Have there been any changes with respect to your results? If so, please write in detail below what caused these changes to transpire. If there has been no change in your ratings, take the time to pray, asking Holy Spirit to speak to you on reasons why. Journal what you receive below.

CHAPTER SEVEN

The Unveiling of the Coming Age

Break The Dams – Release The River

"Blow the trumpet in Zion, and sound an alarm
on My holy mountain. For the day of the
Lord is coming, for it is at hand."
Joel 2:1 (NKJV)

Winds of change will sweep the earth

We are living in one of the most historic and meaningful seasons this planet has ever hosted, and as we come to the close of our time together in this book, I wish to inspire you with what I see awaiting us on God's heavenly schedule for you and planet Earth. In our key scripture, we see that the prophet Joel was stunned in his day as the Lord opened his eyes to a coming season where the earth would be swept with great shaking, urgency and outpouring. My heart in sharing all this teaching with you (as instructed by God) was in leading you to this moment. You are being prepared for such a season that is coming upon the earth. A time of great shaking in the church and systems of this world, where routines and regularities we have grown comfortable with will be shaken and displaced. We will either wrestle with the winds of change and grow weary, or adapt our sail to accommodate this new direction and embark on new shores of supernatural release. Those who desire to be established in present truth as Peter once encouraged the church to do will be busy demonstrating (2 Peter 1:12), while those who are fighting over old norms will be busy deliberating. There will be a clear distinction with one antagonizing the other, but the former will remain steadfast, occupied by the mission and mind of Christ. They will do great exploits and indulge in great manifestations of the glory unlike what the church has ever seen!

This pattern in the church will be mirrored in the marketplace, as great displacement comes to corporations and entities who have long been mountains in the marketplace. The Lord will indeed level mountains and raise valleys, and new technological, pharmaceutical and environmental players will enter the market. Be sober of the marriage of technology with the pharmaceutical entity. Out of their belly will come new practices made public under the umbrella of advancement, and it will cause great contentions amongst the people, but a unified voice shall delay the schemes of infanticide and the unborn tragedy and stir up revised governmental activity. When you see the rise of gas giants such as Exxon in 2026, and the following appearance of the summer eclipse, you will know that the rain to displace has already begun.

The whore who rides upon the mountain of media will also be thrown from her high place as Jezebel was thrown out of her tower (2 Kings 9:33-35), and this mountain will vomit up their own undoings unlike any time that has transpired before. Great distrust shall arise amongst players in the entertainment industry, and many will abandon former alliances. This will be a sign to my people that their voice must rise with the tide. This is the time to strike in the sickle and reap the lost from the blinding mist of worldly despair. He who has ears to hear, let him hear.

> "Arise, shine; For your light has come! And the glory of the Lord is risen upon you. For behold, the darkness shall cover the earth, And deep darkness the people; But the Lord will arise over you, And His glory will be seen upon you. The Gentiles shall come to your light, And kings to the brightness of your rising."
>
> Isaiah 60:1-3

Friends, this is not an hour to be afraid but to be ready! The Lord also showed me vessels of incredible light piercing the darkness just as Isaiah prophesied in the scripture above, and souls being saved in droves. The harvest has never been as plentiful as it will be then, and laborers will arise to His calling upon their lives. It will not be business as usual, and cookie cutter methodology and old wine skin evangelical practices will give way to the raw power and love of God manifesting through hearts that are not afraid to be persecuted for His Name's sake.

If you are reading this, I believe that you have been called to join this company of overcomers that God is raising up in this hour. What I shared above is just a sprinkle of prophetic insight concerning what I believe is to come, but the greater story is the continual rise of God's people as we co-labor to make the kingdoms of this world the kingdoms of our Lord and His Christ (Revelation 11:15). Therefore, don't shrink back in utilizing the gifts God has given you for impact. Begin to whet the axe head with use (Ecclesiastes 10:10), and stir up the gifts (2 Timothy 1:6) so that you might grow in greater discernment and demonstration (Hebrews 5:14) in these days that will be a precursor to what is to come. Let's give further instruction on how you can win in this way, readying yourself for the unveiling of the coming age.

THE APOSTOLIC EXAMPLE

One of the major responsibilities for Apostles is establishing right foundations for the church and fathering them into a place of maturity. As we prepare to close out this book, my heart as an Apostle is to impart to you spiritual capacity to do what God has called you to do. The Apostle Paul's relationship with his spiritual son Timothy gives us great insight into how this works, and we would be wise to reflect upon their example.

> "Therefore I remind you to stir up the gift of God which is in you through the laying on of my hands. For God has not given us a spirit of fear, but of power and of love and of a sound mind."
>
> 2 Timothy 1:6-7

1. The reminder to stir up the gift

Paul understands the weakness of mens' souls, as we so easily become distracted. We often need to be reminded so that we can be sharpened, and it is good to have relationships around you that can sharpen you in this way (Proverbs 27:17). Genuine people that remind you of your potential in God, and hold you to account in walking it out. I want to take this opportunity right now to remind you today to recall God's prophetic promises and impartations over your life, and bring them to your remembrance.

2. The impartation from his hands

Paul allows us to know that what has been imparted to Timothy has been released through delegated, God-ordained authority and sanctioning. This grants validation and confidence for the exercising of what has been given, and releases authority. We do not want to be as the sons of Sceva in Acts 19:13-20, who were embarrassed by spiritual forces because they were not connected authentically in relationship with Christ, and authorized by Holy Spirit through the church. Please be certain to stay connected to Christ's Church. We do not need lone rangers functioning outside of Godly sanction and accountability. It has brought too much damage to the church already. Stay connected to the hands that cover you, that you might receive some impartation to grow in the increase of what God desires to do. My spiritual father who wrote the foreword to this book, has always been there to impart and encourage me, as well as hold me accountable. We need more fathers like these who are not manipulative, religious or egotistical, but humble, connected and powerful.

EVICTING THE SPIRIT OF FEAR

Paul continues in 2 Timothy 1:7 to expose the spirit of fear that diminishes the gifts and overall, he reveals not just to Timothy, but also to us how we are to whet our axes in the midst of such opposition. The axe represents our spiritual gifts, and whetting the axe (the practice of sharpening the blade - Ecclesiastes 10:10) is done by possessing revelation, embracing activation and humbly submitting to the process of evaluation. The word used for *spirit* in the greek can also be translated as *wind* or a *blast of wind*, and you will see that in the headlines below. Let us journey together into these three areas as we close, and as I pray for God to sweep over you with a spiritual blast of His power, love and soundness of mind.

WHETTING THE AXE (SPIRITUAL GIFT) BY REVELATION

A spirit/blast of power

The word power here is the greek word **dunamis**. This speaks of miraculous power or power that enables the supernatural. It also speaks of possessing the ability to act. In order to believe by faith for boldness and specifics in our prophetic release, we must be confident in the power that dwells in us. That we have been blasted with supernatural power! Luke 10:19 reminds us that Jesus has given us all power over every serpent and scorpion, and that includes the spirit of fear or the blast of fear the enemy sends when God wants to use us mightily as we step out to give witness of

His abundant life. We must speak to the tempest of fear and quiet it with our God-given authority. Also, our continual and increased submission to walking in faith and functioning in power, equates to greater levels of authority being released in us over time (Matthew 25:21).

A spirit/blast of love

This is love that grants us security in our service to others. It protects us from the spirit of fear as directed towards men, and how they will respond to us as we step out. This fear promotes compromises and acts as a limiter to the move of Holy Spirit's graces in us. Like the limiter in your car, it stops you from reaching your full potential because it worships soulish conservatism above faith activated propulsion. Soulish conservatism says, "Let me not take the risk; I might miss it," while faith-activated propulsion says, "God have Your way. I trust Your leadership!" Remember, you have been given a spirit of love, and the one who possesses such love has full assurance and security in the One who extends such a grace, and that is God, our Father. So how does one whet his axe with such revelation? By not being afraid, and stepping out of every box of limitations the enemy tries to put on you or you upon yourself. Perfect love casts out all fear (1 John 4:18)!

Interestingly, one of my first encounters with the demonic was in a dream at the beginning of my Christian journey. I was walking up a hill towards an amazing church filled with light at the very top. Many were also walking up his hill, and outside was quite dark. As I trod on upward, a child grabbed me and tried to converse with me. The little boy kept trying to tell me that I was wasting my time and my activity made no sense. Immediately in the dream I discerned this was not a child as it would seem, but a demonic distraction. I placed my right hand on the child's head and began to command the demon to leave. The skin of the child then melted off its face and a reptile looking creature with the most hideous features was before me. It tried to hiss and intimidate me once more but the scripture of 1 John 4:18 came to mind and I opened my mouth once more to declare it. "Perfect love casts out all fear!" The creature then completely dissolved and I continued my journey up towards the lit church on the hilltop. Let's be empowered by God's spiritual blast of love over our lives!

A spirit/blast of discipline (sound mind)

The Greek word for *sound mind* denotes one who understands or is able to perceive what is best, and restrains or releases him/herself accordingly. This is divine wisdom which grants success, and paints a picture of someone possessing meekness. As pertaining to the prophetic, it speaks of timeliness and not being anxious or overzealous concerning sharing what God has given. We must be bold enough to say what God would have us to speak, yet we must also be wise concerning how we share and if it is to be shared. This comes through maturity in the Word and intimacy with God, as we study to examine His heart and methodology in addressing matters. Many are afraid to go deeper in their prophetic release and do not **dare to share** because they are not confident that what they perceive is accurate or worth being said. At such a point, one must bring the soulish mind under subjection to the will of Holy Spirit, thus allowing God to be **glorified in fullness**. Again, as you grow in the Word and allow your spirit to be fed with God's wisdom through His Word, confidence comes in this area.

If God has invested in us these attributes through His Son, we must be confident to walk as Jesus walked (1 John 2:6). For by His tender mercies, He has granted us the power that

It's time for impact!

confirms authority, the love that ensures security, and the discipline that authenticates maturity. Therefore, let us shake off the dust (fears, intimidation, unworthiness, slothfulness) and arise in boldness and accuracy in our prophetic gifting and other spiritual gifts (Isaiah 52:2). It's time for impact!

WHETTING THE AXE (SPIRITUAL GIFT) BY ACTIVATION

As God's prophetic messenger, you have been called to speak for Him with distinction, nobility and accuracy as mentioned in Chapter 3. However, let us look closer at the area of accuracy. Accuracy speaks of the quality or state of being correct or precise. It lends to the idea of performing a task not necessarily with perfection, but with precision. As a former basketball shooting guard, I know what it is to be under the pressure or demand for accuracy. My role on the team was to shoot the basketball, and obviously score. My coach designed plays just so that I could be open to shoot, and all of the other players on the court worked in symmetry to ensure I was given that opportunity. As everyone executed their role, I had to ensure that the shot taken was accurate; to miss would be to negate the hard work everyone had put in to make the opportunity available for the shot. How did I ensure that my teammates and coach could count on me to score? I practiced, and practiced hard! I would spend weeks shooting at least 300 shots per day, as well as strengthening my shoulders and arms through weight training. This measure of training caused my gift to excel and though I didn't score 100% of the time when I shot the basketball, I did score often enough to be valued for the position I held on the team. Why am I sharing this story with you? Well, to teach us two fundamentals that God deems necessary for activating our spiritual man.

Pressure and practice

Let's hear from Apostle James as he addresses the issue of pressure.

> "Consider it a sheer gift, friends, when tests and challenges come at you from all sides. You know that under pressure, your faith-life is forced into the open and shows its true colors. So don't try to get out of anything prematurely. Let it do its work so you become mature and well-developed, not deficient in any way."

> James 1:2, 4 (MSG)

I love this rendition of James and I believe it speaks for itself. Just as how my shoulder and arm muscles needed that weight training to grow and become stronger, so must we embrace the pressure that comes our way. It is part of our building process, and we must use it to whet our axe by activating and stirring up our faith in the midst of it. With regards to flowing in the prophetic, do not stay on the shore where you are comfortable but step out of the boat and allow God to stretch and mature your faith. I recall there was a student of mine who was excited and desirous of being stretched in an activation during my time of conducting prophetic training in one of our spiritual gifts development modules. As I was beginning the activation, I shared with the class that I would not make it too difficult but out of his mouth came these words, "Why not? Stretch me!" On hearing these words, others in the class grew disgruntled; they were quite happy with having it easy. However, I did go ahead and stretched his faith along with the others, and out of 23 attempts to speak an accurate word of knowledge to a person standing behind him (he had to call the name of the nation that was on the mind of the person), he was precise and hit the mark 21 out of those 23 times! The others came in around 17 to 19 out of 23, which is by all means still excellent. However, God honored his faith and he only got it wrong twice. From this example, we see how we can become mature through embracing pressure. Practice also sharpens our gifting, as long as we are under right authority and covering, pushing ourselves to the limit. This is what Paul was referring to by using the words "stir up". Remember King David when he was but a boy? He stirred up his sling shot gift with the lions and the bears as he shepherded his father's flock. God then used this same gift that was fine-tuned and accurate to set a stone in Goliath's head with precision, slaying the giant (1 Samuel 17:49). Beloved, there are giants in peoples' lives and God wants to raise up a prophetic company that will be precise, polished and sharp. Like David the prophet, we will be proficient in our gifting, ready both in and out of season (2 Timothy 4:2), as vessels fit for the

Master's use. However, as we become proficient and confident (1 Samuel 17:34-40), we must understand that our utter dependency is upon the Holy Spirit who brings the revelation to our spirits, as proportionate to our faith (1 Samuel 17:47, Romans 12:6).

WHETTING THE AXE (SPIRITUAL GIFT) BY EVALUATION

Is my axe head really dull? As you can see from the previous story with the eager and apathetic students, pressure reveals to us where we are at. Therefore in order to grow in the gifting God gives you, it is fundamental to allow this process of evaluation. We must come to grips with where we are at, always seeking to grow into greater depths in our spiritual journey with the Lord. Besides through pressure, evaluation comes in three major ways:

- **Evaluation directly from Holy Spirit (1 Corinthians 2:9-16, 13:12, John 14:16-17, 26)**

He has come to lead you into all truth. Allow Him permission to search you and expose anything that may be in the way of you going deeper in the things of God (Psalm 139:23-24). He will also affirm you of where you're going right and concerning what you're doing well, so don't just listen for correction but soak in His affirmation.

- **Evaluation from God's delegated authority (The biblical epistles, 2 Timothy 1:5, Titus)**

We spoke of this earlier and stressed its significance so I will simply remind you to stay connected! Satan hates a united Kingdom, and we need the spirit of Elijah now more than ever as Malachi prophesied, where the hearts of the fathers are turned to the children, and the children to the fathers (Malachi 4:5-6). Fight to stay in fellowship where God has planted you, because that is where you will grow and flourish the most (Psalm 92:13-15).

- **Evaluation from God latently communicating.**

I refer to this as latent language. This is when God uses people unknown or known to you to communicate for Him unknowing to them. For example, having a conversation where the other person is not necessarily speaking concerning something biblical but Holy Spirit highlights a statement in that conversation and directs it towards you. It brings confirmation, conviction or revelation concerning God's heart towards the receiver. This is also a method by which one can be open for evaluation.

Keep Your Axe Head Sharp

As you allow these three processes of revelation, activation and evaluation in your life, you will remain on the cutting edge of God's purposes, being ready for every good work. In spite of all the enemy may do to deter you, don't allow your passion to wane, but allow the grace of God to be the oil in your engine and the gas in your tank. Stay sharp and keep going!

Spring Up O Well!

In Numbers 21, we see a new generation being pruned and raised up to believe God for His fullness in their lives. The older generation that did not believe God was dying off in the wilderness, as many of them were killed by fiery serpents just a few moments into this chapter because of their unbelief and complaining. A brazen serpent had to be lifted on a staff to heal them, and this was no doubt a symbolic representation of the coming Christ who would take on our sins and the judgement demanded for our healing. Without the best example of faith being exemplified by these older ones, the new generation was having to mark out its path of obedience to press toward the promise. As they traversed onward, they left the eastern Arnon Valley and moved on to a place called Beer (meaning a well, Numbers 21:18). Here it is recalled that under the leadership of Moses, the people had gathered together and God supernaturally gave them water from a well. Therefore they all lyrically celebrated that blessing and opened their voices in a poetic song, admonishing each other to sing to the well—"Spring Up O Well!". It was a song of confident expectation that shifted the tide of Israel's attitude toward God. They saw God as the One who is faithful to His own, and they drew forth the water with joy. Interestingly, the prophet Isaiah also saw a prophetic preview of what we would experience in Christ, and he prophesied that there would be a people who with joy would draw water from the wells of salvation (Isaiah 12:3). He goes on to say that they shall sing and shout for joy (Isaiah 12:6). Friends, I want you to know that Isaiah was seeing you and me, with joy participating in and receiving from the fullness of all Christ has purchased for us through His suffering. As we come to a close and with all that you have received, I pray that as you leave these pages you will take with you fiery impartation that will empower you to turn this world right-side up for Jesus! May your song rise to Jesus in worship daily, the wellspring of your life.

As He invited the Samaritan woman in John 4:14, He also invites us to draw from His well this day. For it is only then that our well will be filled, and out of us will flow a fountain of water that will spring up into everlasting life, impacting the lives of others. Remember, information without application only serves to make you a modern day Pharisee. With what you know now, you cannot afford to live a life of faith without works (James 2:26). Like the older generation who missed the mark, this will result in death and not seeing the promises of God. Rather, be a part of the new generation of believers God is raising up. This generation is not characterized by an age metric (how old or young you are), but only by your belief and confident expectation in God. Rise up in faith, and go into your world as a powerhouse for heaven and a major problem for hell. Prophesy purpose into broken hearts! Heal the sick, raise the dead, cleanse those who have disease, and drive out demons (Matthew 10:8, Mark 16:17-18). Freely you have received; go now and freely give; I am praying for you. Let us all arise to be part of God's new generation!

About the Author

Dwayne Howard is the Senior Pastor of Awake The Flame Ministries in North Miami, Florida. As a graduate of Christian International Ministry Training College founded by Dr. Bill Hamon, he serves as an ordained Apostle and licensed minister in their Apostolic Network, which covers thousands of apostolic, pastoral, missionary and prophetic leaders across the globe. He trains, counsels and mentors persons of varying spheres ranging from business to the pulpit, is a John Maxwell Certified Coach, a Bible School teacher, business director, and licensed counselor. Dwayne is foremost a family man, happily married to his wife, Tao, and a proud father of three sons. Above all, he desires to see a passion for Jesus stirred in the hearts of all men.

Complementary eCourses

For those who desire further equipping, we offer an eCourse to complement this book. You can visit ecourse.awaketheflame.com and sign up there. The *Spring Up O Well* interactive course consists of eight 60 minute recorded sessions with Apostle Dwayne Howard, and upon registering you will have lifetime access to the material provided.

If you are new to the prophetic we would also strongly recommend our eCourse, *Competent To Prophesy*. It is our foundational course in functioning in your prophetic gifting, and will be helpful as you grow in your calling. Prior to this book release, we have for the last 15 years equipped hundreds via our *Competent To Prophesy* course. This course also comes with its own manual, and upon registration you will be given lifetime access to the material provided therein.

Another exciting offering is our *Dreams, Visions & Spiritual Encounters* eCourse which provides a biblical guide to understanding the visual realm of encounter. For over ten years, Apostle Dwayne has been teaching and equipping hundreds of believers in the Body of Christ to rightly interpret and better understand the dreams they dream, visions they perceive, and encounters they have experienced

in the Lord, all from a biblical perspective and with the purpose of encouraging intimacy with Jesus. Dreams and visions have always been instrumental to God revealing Himself to His people (Job 33:14-18), and this course will help you discover how critical it is to you.

Please feel free to peruse our website for further information, and to view our other course offerings. May Christ's water of abundant life spring up out of the well of your life.

Awake The Flame Ministries

Awake The Flame Ministries is called to awaken passion for Jesus in the nations of the Earth. We have a burning desire to serve others in discovering their identity, fulfilling their purpose, accessing their true potential, and walking out a life of fulfillment in Christ. Our mandate is ignited by God's promise in Isaiah 42:3, which reveals the tenderness of Jesus towards His chosen. The bruised reed He promises not to break, and the flickering flame He declares will not be quenched. This declaration of commitment from the Lord reveals His heart towards us, and we desire all men to encounter such love, especially the battered, the bruised and the broken. By revealing the love and passion of Jesus for His people, our confidence is that in turn many hearts would awake in corresponding love and passion towards Jesus, the Desire of the Nations. Such a people will be transformed internally and empowered holistically to impact their spheres of influence in every fabric of society.

awaketheflame.com

info@awaketheflame.com | 888.850.2836 (ATFM)

@awake.the.flame | @awaketheflame